TOMATO COOKING AROUND THE WORLD

The Love Apple Cookbook

Apples of Love

TOMATO COOKING AROUND THE WORLD

The Love Apple Cookbook

Don Bevona

GRAMERCY PUBLISHING COMPANY · NEW YORK

Contents

Acknowledgments

That great warrior Hernando Cortés is possibly the first man to whom homage is due for the discovery of the tomato, that noble vegetable which inspired this book. His ruthless conquest of Mexico resulted in the introduction of the tomato to European tables and its subsequent enrichment of cooking the world over.

My personal thanks go to those others who have encouraged and aided me in the writing of this book: they include another "warrior" (a little less formidable than Cortés), Dan Morris; Thomas Browne Bennett, whose passion for tomatoes is equal only to mine; Walter Hamshar, former Marine Editor of the New York *Herald Tribune;* John Brimer, author and editor; my cousin and fellow epicure, Jim Toriello, owner of the renowned Amalfi Restaurant in New York City; Herb Strum, of the United States Department of Agriculture's Plentiful Foods Program; my wife's grandparents, the late Julius and Julia Roth; the United Fresh Fruit and Vegetable Association; William D. Brown of W. Atlee Burpee Co.; the California Artichoke Advisory Board; the South African Rock Lobster Service Corporation; the International Shrimp Council; the Spice Trade Association; the American Lamb Council; the National Broiler Council; the Bourbon Institute; and the New York Botanical Garden Society. All have been most generous in giving assistance in their various ways toward the preparation of this book.

I

The Tomato Becomes
the Love Apple

L ove may make the world go around with the pleasant
motion of a pink carousel but when it crossed the path
of the delicious, albeit innocent, tomato it threw the poor vegetable into a spin. Because the spin lasted from the start of the
16th to the middle of the 19th century, the tomato still plays
only an insignificant part in the famous cuisines of northern
Europe.

Love is thought to be the cause of this unpopularity because the notion got around that the simple garden tomato
somehow provoked man's sexual desires to an inordinate degree. The fruit of the tomato vine was considered an aphrodisiac and in France tomatoes were at one time even used as
love tokens. Mostly because of this outrageous slander, tomatoes were long viewed by many people in northern Europe as
dangerous though ornamental plants.

The fault, as far as one can tell, lies with the early European botanists, then called herbalists. Such famous men as

Mattioli and Rembert Dodoens were the first to investigate the plant which came to Europe from the New World as a result of Hernando Cortés' remarkable conquest of Mexico. Some of the early observations about the strange flora were fairly accurate, but a passion for classification led the investigators astray; for they found similarities between the innocent tomato vine and any number of poisonous plants.

Many early botanists experimented with the leaves as well as with the fruit of the new plants. They boiled them, steeped them, and sometimes distilled the liquids obtained. These concoctions were then used for pharmaceutical purposes in line with the medical practices of the times. The early herbalists believed that each plant had some physical characteristic which gave a clue to its curative properties. Onions, for instance, with their hollow, tubelike stems, were looked upon as being good to cure any illness of the throat.

Nicholas Culpeper, the famous English herbalist, in *The English Physician and Herbal,* written about 1653, noted that by the "icon or image of every herb, man first found out their virtues." He observed that the herb *Polygonatum biflorum,* or Solomon's Seal, which is distinguished by circular scars on its root stalk, was useful in mending broken bones and that "it soldereth and glues together bones in a very short space of time."

No one quite knows what sign led the herbalists to label the tomato a love potion. But the United States Department of Agriculture has conducted experiments with the leaves of the tomato plant and discovered that they contain crystalline *Matadine* from which sex hormones can be, and are, manufactured. This might partially explain why the early herbalists believed the plant to contain such remarkable powers. Of course we can't be certain that they knew this.

The tomato has been used as the basis of numerous soaps and lotions for years because its mild acidity has a beneficial effect upon the skin. The cosmetic use of this acid might well have added to the mystique of the tomato's role as an aid to love.

To many women a lovelier skin ensures a more interesting

love life. Beauty-conscious European women have been wash-
ing their faces with love apple soap and applying tomato
lotions as a skin treatment for centuries. The soft, luxuriously
rich lather created by tomato soap is a wonderful aid in main-
taining a young, glowing skin tone. Tomato soap imported
from Italy can be purchased in chic boutiques everywhere.
The soap often comes in the shape of a tomato. The lotions,
however, can be easily made at home.

LOVE APPLE SKIN LOTION

⅓ cup fresh tomato juice, extracted without pulp or seeds
    (approx. 1 large tomato)
⅓ cup fresh lime juice, strained
⅓ cup glycerine, or olive oil

Chop the tomatoes fine. Place a large, clean piece of linen
over a small bowl. Cover the cloth with the tomatoes. Gently
gather up the linen so that a ball is formed with the tomatoes
inside the cloth. Squeeze so that the tomato juice is extracted
without the pulp. Squeeze limes and pour the juice through a
fine sieve. Combine all ingredients. The lotion will keep for
weeks in the refrigerator.

In former times olive oil was used instead of glycerine,
and rose water was used instead of the citrus acid from the
lime. This lotion can be made with canned ingredients, but be
certain to use dietetic tomato juice without salt.

But there are other more popular theories which explain
the term "love apple" which was soon the *nom de guerre* of
the tomato.

The fascinating story of this oft-squeezed, squashed, and
otherwise ill-fondled fruit began with Christopher Columbus
and the discovery of the New World. That momentous occa-
sion was the start of a wild, glorious love affair between man
and the tomato which has been carried on ever since with
impassioned abandon. Cortés and the conquistadores who
were in Mexico avidly seeking gold came upon the slightly
acid, sweet-fleshed tomato in the Aztec gardens. Called

Xtomatles (see-toh-mah-tles) by the Aztecs, it is easy to see whence came the root of our modern word "tomato."

This odd plant apparently made little impression on the Spaniards who called it *manzanas* because of its apple-like appearance. The first tomatoes had a yellow, rather than a red cast, and were small and berry-like. In seeking riches the conquistadores discovered a far more precious bounty, that of the golden tomato. But for many years after its discovery the plants languished in Spanish gardens, valued only as ornamental vines instead of for their edible fruit.

Little did Cortés imagine the benefits and glories to be conferred on cookery or how greatly changed would be the world's eating habits because of his conquests. But the tomato's long journey might have come to naught, according to some accounts, were it not for a Spanish trader who brought some of the curious *manzanas* seeds to a friend in Italy.

Although the tomato by this time was being examined by many learned herbalists to discover its properties, some poor Spaniards and Italians were blithely eating the tasty fruit of the strange apple vine. Since the Spaniards were also known in Europe as the Moors, the Italian who first planted the seeds in his garden called the round, red berry *Pomo del Moro* or Moor's apple. This name was further changed because of the tomato's original yellow color to *pomo d'oro*, or golden apple, the present Italian name for the tomato.

While the tomato was being joyously and lovingly carried from Italian gardens to Italian saucepans, a slip of the lip sent the vegetable on one of the strangest paths in culinary history. According to the legend, a romantic Frenchman visiting an Italian family around this time asked his host what the strange new apple was.

"*Pomi dei Moro,*" he was told, "Moor's Apples."

This to the Frenchman sounded exactly like *Pomme d'amour*, which in French is "love apple." Thus the tomato was introduced into France as a "love apple" and through this aphrodisiacal title, along with strange reports from herbalists such as Mattioli, became identified as a food which offered much more than good nutrition.

Mattioli in 1554 listed the *mala aurea,* or golden apple, as he called the tomato, among a class of sinister narcotic herbs such as belladonna, henbane, nightshade and mandrake. Powerful drugs made from these strange plants had unusual or even deadly effects upon the human system. Ignorant diners, thus warned by the leading scientific lights of their day against enjoying the love apple as a food, shunned it—after all, who knew what powerful or deadly drug lay in that tempting berry?

But despite the sad manner in which circumstance and love had turned away the tomato from the world's dinner tables, the luscious fruit has at last made its way into our kitchens as a magnificent food and a delight to the stomach. Cooks have become so enamored of the tomato, and their devotion is so great that hundreds upon hundreds of superb tomato dishes have been created and more will no doubt come along. This book is an open love letter to the tomato. Its aim is to offer further delicious nuances to the culinary use of the tomato by means of unusual and tasty recipes.

II

Salads and Appetizers

The introduction of strange new plants from an unknown world beyond the seas sent herbalists in Merrie Old England into a flurry of activity. All over the island kingdom spades flashed in the sun and hoes cultivated row upon row of this exotic greenery.

These learned men specialized in the medicinal aspect of botany. They studied the known listings of different plants in their early botanical books (called "herbals") so that they could examine and then classify the herbs of the New World with those of the Old. This scientific activity not only spurred vegetable gardening but created advances in agriculture which eventually resulted in the production of summer fruits during the winter months.

The herbalists soon found that the harsh English climate killed tender plants, and they moved the more delicate varieties to special gardening sheds which they called "greenhouses." The greenhouse in the Apothecaries Garden in Chelsea was heated in 1684 by means of glowing embers placed in a hole in the floor. The warm air, botanists discovered, helped the plants to live longer. The adoption in 1717 of glass roofs for these heated greenhouses made possible the cultivation of plants which could not stand the English climate, even during the summer months. The botanists soon found that they could create a viable atmosphere in January by controlled heat, and the first hothouse was soon developed.

Hothouses were improved over the years and they are now capable of producing fresh vegetables under the most adverse climatic conditions, and very economically too. Much of Iceland's fresh produce is home grown in hothouses, and Belgium's farmers, whose northern climate is too severe for delicate fruits, have had great success with hothouses—so much so that Belgium's hothouse grapes are much in demand throughout northern Europe.

In the United States hothouses played an important part in the cultivation of the *lycopersicon esculentum,* the tender tomato vine, particularly during winter months when its delicious fruit was very rare indeed. Winter-chilled Easterners were especially grateful when early American hothouses supplied fresh tomatoes for their tables.

As transportation improved, fresh winter tomatoes were sent to Eastern markets from Mexico and the southern states. The hothouse varieties, while still salable, were sold in decreasing quantities. Most of the fresh winter tomatoes sold in the North are grown in the golden southern sun and are thus country fresh for our tables.

Like all raw fruits, tomatoes are at their very best when served in season because they can be vine ripened and delivered to market without traveling thousands of miles. During winter months tomato-starved people who crave the full flavor of the fresh fruit are often disappointed with supermarket tomatoes. The reason for this disappointment stems from the fact that tomato growers take great pains to make sure their produce travels well and arrives in an edible condition. This means that the tomatoes are not packed rosy-red because they would rot before reaching stores thousands of miles away.

For a long time I wondered what could be done about these supermarket tomatoes until I learned the secret of bringing winter tomatoes to the peak of flavor from Cherry Joe, an old Italian fruit and vegetable dealer in New York City.

"Tomatoes like to go to sleep in the dark. Then they wake up very, very delicious. Try it and you'll see," he advised me.

Cherry Joe knew that since winter tomatoes are sold in supermarkets with just a tinge of pink, instead of the full flush of crimson, they have to be ripened further, and in a very special way.

Tomatoes are usually sold in cellopane-wrapped packages of three or four. When you arrive home with the groceries, remove the fruit from the cellophane and check to see that there are no soft spots which might cause the fruit to rot. Then place the fruit in a bowl and put it "to sleep" in a dark closet. Some fussy tomato eaters have been known to wrap each tomato individually before putting them in the closet. In any case, make sure that the closet is a convenient one. If you tuck the tomatoes away in some infrequently used cabinet, the chances are that they will be forgotten. This is a particular fault of mine. (Such a memory lapse is invariably noticed several weeks later by some astonished member of the household who chances upon the malodorous mass of putrescent vegetable matter resting among the company tea service.) Smell and feel the tomatoes daily to see if they are improving. Your nose is the best guide to a ripe tomato. When it smells like summer, devour it.

Cherry tomatoes can be another way to capture the flavorful perfection of summertime during the frost season. Gourmets who want a true vine-ripened tomato taste when snow is on the ground always pick up a basket of cherry tomatoes at the market. A cherry tomato needs no ripening because for some marvelous, though unknown, reason nature has endowed this tiny love apple with all the luscious flavor of a summer's day. These miniatures are an excellent base on which to build a winter salad that in taste is about as close as one can get to one using in-season tomatoes.

The culinary appeal of the love apple is enhanced because it is both a vegetable and a fruit—a vegetable when served cooked and a fruit when served uncooked. Among fruits it is classed as a berry because it is non-shedding, has pulp, and contains one or more seeds which are not stones. Because of this unusual make-up the tomato can be cooked in many different ways. No other food is as widely used in cooking today. The tomato is the master of the salad, both hot and cold, and has been crowned not only king of fruits but emperor among vegetables. Without the grace of this almost perfect vegetable-fruit, the modern menu may appear woefully lacking.

Salads, many feel, were the first tomato dishes to be devised, because the venturesome Europeans who first tasted the strange new berry thought it exceedingly delicious and added it to their salads for variety. Soon salads were planned around the tomato. Americans in northern states were tomato-shy for a long time, but when they first ate it, the tomato was raw and in salads.

Julia Davis Roth, of Westhampton, Long Island, who was descended from the seafaring Davis family which first settled that part of the United States, had among her treasured recipes many tomato dishes. This salad recipe, which is at least one hundred years old, is presented (with a few modern revisions) as Grandma Roth put it down in her "receipt" book.

❧ TOMATO NASTURTIUM SALAD ❧

5 large ripe tomatoes   *Salad cream**
Fresh red or yellow nastur-
*   tium blossoms, unsprayed*

Peel the tomatoes without scalding. Slice them in ½-inch thick rounds. Put them on ice or refrigerate until well chilled. Arrange chilled tomatoes on a serving platter. Garnish with

nasturtium blossoms, and generously spoon on salad cream.
Serve immediately.

SERVES 6

* SALAD CREAM

4 hard-cooked egg yolks	*1 tsp. mild prepared mus-*
6 Tbs. heavy cream	*tard*
	¼ tsp. salt

Rub the egg yolks through a very fine sieve. To them, add the
cream, mustard, and salt. Mix well until dressing is smooth.
Add more cream as necessary to bring dressing to a creamy,
pouring consistency.

America came into its own in food and drink during the
latter part of the 19th century when the bounty of the land
helped change the simple pioneer tastes of our forebears.
One of the most interesting of all early American tomato
salads testifies to the Gay-Nineties pre-Prohibition love of fine
wine, hearty beefsteak tomatoes, and pleasant seasonings. This
easily made yet delicious salad borders on the sublime when
served with a thick, juicy steak.

ᴥ§ OLD TIME SALOON SALAD §ᴥ

2 large beefsteak tomatoes	*4 Tbs. grated parmesan*
1 cup extra-dry white wine	*cheese*
	4 Tbs. good light olive oil

Core the beefsteak tomatoes and cut into thick wedges. Place
the wedges in a deep salad bowl, and pour the wine over them.
Let marinate in the refrigerator for 10 minutes. Then sprinkle
with the cheese and oil. Toss very lightly. Chill in coldest part
of your refrigerator for 45 minutes.

SERVES 4

Tomatoes go well with artichokes. Artichokes have been culinary favorites since the time of Queen Dido, who ate even the leaves of the plant, preferred in those early times to the edible flower buds we today know as artichokes. After several thousand years of hearty artichoke eating it was discovered that there were certain parts of the bud which were tastier than the rest; they were the hearts and bottoms of the tasty vegetable. Gourmets found these to be delicious when removed from the bulk of the artichoke and served in a salad.

⋖§ ARTICHOKE AND TOMATO SALAD §⋗

6 cooked artichoke hearts or
*   bottoms, sliced in halves*
½ cup French dressing, con-
*   taining chopped chervil*
*   or parsley*

6 small tomatoes
Fresh chopped parsley for
*   garnish*

If frozen artichoke hearts are used, cook according to directions on the package, and cool before using. Artichoke bottoms are available, already cooked and packed in water in 15-oz. cans, on most supermarket shelves. Arrange the hearts or bottoms on a small platter, and pour over them one-half of the French dressing. Cut the tomatoes into thin slices. Arrange a layer of tomatoes on top of artichokes and top with remainder of dressing. Garnish with fresh parsley.

SERVES 4

Artichokes are so versatile that they can be easily adapted to any number of meals and served in many different ways. They are excellent when combined with tomato juice in aspic and used for a very special holiday dinner or luncheon entree. The great French chef Antonin Carême observed that in preparing a cold table only two aspic colors should be used—one clear and one of a vivid hue, such as tomato-red.

ARTICHOKE AND TOMATO ASPIC

1 Tbs. (1 envelope) unfla-
  vored gelatin
1¾ cups tomato juice
¼ tsp. red hot sauce
1 Tbs. vinegar
1 Tbs. lemon juice
½ tsp. celery salt
½ tsp. onion salt
¼ tsp. dry mustard
⅛ tsp. pepper

4 medium-sized artichokes
2 Tbs. lemon juice
1 tsp. salt
DRESSING:
¼ cup mayonnaise
1 Tbs. grated onion
¼ tsp. red hot sauce
¼ tsp. dry mustard
Salt and pepper
Chicory

Soften gelatin in ½ cup tomato juice. Add remaining tomato
juice, ¼ tsp. red hot sauce, vinegar, 1 tbs. lemon juice, celery
salt, onion salt, ¼ tsp. dry mustard and pepper. Blend. Cook
over a low heat for 10 minutes, stirring frequently. Pour the
tomato mixture into 4 individual molds (½ cup capacity each).
Chill until firm.

While mixture is chilling, wash artichokes, trim stems to
1-inch, pull off tough outer leaves, and snip off tips of remaining leaves. Place artichokes in 1 inch of boiling water,
to which 2 tbs. lemon juice have been added. Sprinkle ¼ tsp.
salt over each artichoke. Cover tightly and cook for 20–45
minutes or until stems can be easily pierced (depending upon
the size of the artichokes). Remove artichokes and turn upside down immediately to drain. Chill.

Combine mayonnaise, onion, ¼ tsp. red hot sauce, ¼ tsp.
dry mustard, and salt and pepper to taste. Mix well. Unmold
tomato aspic. Garnish with chicory. Serve with dressing and
artichokes.

SERVES 4

Fried tomatoes are dazzling hot appetizers which many a
cook prides himself on. Many another cook finds it difficult to
prepare them properly because they often become soggy. The
trick for a crisp fried tomato is to use a batter to which no
fresh eggs have been added. An easy way to get an eggless

batter in a hurry is to use packaged pancake mix and blend it with milk. The results will be perfectly crisp tomatoes, fit for a king's table.

❧ FRIED TOMATOES ⮞

3 large, firm tomatoes
Salt
⅔ cup pancake mix

6 Tbs. milk
2 Tbs. grated parmesan cheese
Oil for deep-frying

Core and slice the tomatoes into thick wedges. Sprinkle each wedge lightly with salt. Blend the pancake mix and milk well to form a smooth batter. More milk may be needed, depending upon the mix. Dip tomato wedges into the batter and fry in deep fat (370–380°F.) until golden brown, turning once. Remove with slotted spoon and drain well on napkins or absorbent paper. Sprinkle with parmesan cheese and serve at once.

SERVES 4

Neapolitan fishermen love their tomatoes as well as, or probably better than, any other people alive and use tomatoes in almost everything they eat. They also love spices and the fruits of their catch. When all three are combined in a special hot appetizer, the results are a mouth-watering shellfish dish for those who love to eat well. Though a somewhat time-consuming and complicated platter to prepare, the result is well worth the effort.

❧ MUSSELS NEAPOLITAN STYLE ⮞

2 lbs. mussels
3 Tbs. olive oil
1 large garlic clove
1 6-oz. can tomato paste
2½ cups liquid (mussel liq-
uor plus sufficient water)

½ tsp. oregano
½ tsp. capers
Salt and pepper
Crushed red pepper (op-
tional)

Clean the mussels by scrubbing well with a stiff brush under cold running water. Remove algae, sand and strands of beard-like filament. Soak mussels in cold water for 2 hours. Discard those which float to the top. Fill a large pot with 1½ inches of salted water. Let water come to a boil, and gently add mussels. Cover pot and steam mussels for 3 minutes. Cool and remove mussels from shells. Do this over a pot in order not to waste any mussel liquor. Place mussels in a small bowl, and reserve one half shell for each one. Lay each mussel on a half shell in a shallow baking dish and set aside. Strain mussel liquor through a cheesecloth or hair strainer to remove sand or bits of shell. Reserve liquor for the sauce. Add enough water to liquor to equal 2½ cups.

SAUCE: Heat the oil in a saucepan. Sliver the garlic lengthwise into quarters and brown in the oil. Add the tomato paste and fry for 2 minutes with garlic. Then add mussel liquor and water mixture, oregano, and capers (which should be rinsed and drained well). Simmer, covered, for about 30 minutes. Salt and pepper to taste. Add red crushed pepper if desired, but do not use more than ¼ to ½ tsp. Pour sauce over mussels and bake in preheated oven at 425°F. for 15 minutes. Serve over flat Italian whole wheat biscuits or sliced, toasted Italian bread.

SERVES 4

In Sicily the delicate nectar of fresh tomatoes is so prized that one of the finest tomato salads in the world has been devised by discriminating chefs in order to use this palate tempting quality to best advantage. Combining the summer sweetness of cold plum tomatoes, the fragrance of minced garlic, the unique delicate peppery flavor of basil with light olive oil and mild wine vinegar, it is a tasty salad, extremely quick and easy to make.

Sicilians wanting variety often prepare this basic salad in different ways—omitting garlic and using onions sliced paper thin or substituting water or lemon juice for the vinegar.

◆§ SICILIAN SALAD §◆

1 lb. firm plum tomatoes	*Salt and pepper*
1 garlic clove	*¼ cup light olive oil*
1 sprig fresh basil, or 1 tsp.	*1½ tsp. mild wine vinegar*
dry basil	

Chill the tomatoes well. When they are cold, halve them and place in a deep serving bowl. Mince the garlic clove very fine. Chop the fresh basil coarsely or crumble dry basil between palms of hands. Add garlic and basil to tomatoes and sprinkle with salt and pepper. Pour oil and vinegar over the salad, and allow to marinate in refrigerator for at least 15 minutes before serving.

SERVES 4

Another unusual salad which captures the love apple's freshness in a memorable way is a unique soup-like salad. This cold dish utilizes the delightful all-encompassing juice of freshly-chopped tomatoes, combining it with fresh lemons, onions, minced Pascal celery and parsley.

◆§ FRESH TOMATO COBB §◆

4 cups (6 medium) fresh to-	*1 tsp. salt*
matoes	*¼ tsp. ground black pepper*
½ cup minced Pascal celery	*1 tsp. sugar*
3 tsp. minced fresh onion	*3 slices lemon, cut in half*
4 Tbs. fresh lemon juice	*Chopped fresh parsley*

Wash the tomatoes and chop very fine. Add minced celery, minced onion, lemon juice, salt, black pepper and sugar. Mix well and chill thoroughly. Serve as the first course in bowls like a soup. Garnish each with ½ lemon slice sprinkled with chopped fresh parsley.

SERVES 6

In Panama, where the tomato has been eaten for almost as long as in Mexico, land of its discovery, chefs have prepared a cold fresh tomato salad. This popular salad is often used as a fresh relish because of its slight, pleasant piquancy.

⊷§ PANAMA TOMATO AND §⊷
RADISH SALAD

1 large tomato
2 bunches, or 20 medium-
   size radishes
1 tsp. chopped fresh mint
1 Tbs. finely chopped onion
2 Tbs. lemon juice

2 Tbs. olive oil or salad oil
1 tsp. salt
¼ tsp. ground black pepper
¼ tsp. sugar
Lettuce, optional

Peel the tomato and dice finely. Wash the radishes, and cut off green tops and roots. Slice radishes thin and add to tomatoes. Combine mint, onion, lemon juice, salad oil, salt, pepper, and sugar. Mix well and pour over vegetables. Serve on a bed of lettuce, if desired, or as relish on dinner plate.

SERVES 4

The brilliant green color of young roquette leaves complements the crimson glory of the tomato in a salad as delicious as it is beautiful. Shakespeare called this tender salad herb Rocket. At the greengrocer's it is often known as rugola. Roquette leaves are delicate, so this dish needs a little more time and effort to prepare than one which uses a hardier green leaf such as lettuce or endive.

⊷§ ROQUETTE SALAD §⊷

1 bunch young roquette
3 large, firm tomatoes
1 small onion
¼ cup olive oil

2 Tbs. wine vinegar
Salt and pepper
Fresh basil, about 6 large
   leaves

Cut roots from the roquette, and wash each leaf thoroughly. This is usually a very sandy green so a second rinsing would be wise. Allow leaves to crisp in ice water for 25 minutes or more. Slice the tomatoes into thin lengthwise wedges. Combine roquette leaves and tomatoes in salad bowl. Cut the onion into thin lengthwise slices. Add slices to salad, along with olive oil, vinegar, salt and pepper to taste. With your fingers, gently break the basil leaves and add to salad. Toss gently and serve at once. Roquette leaves will wilt very rapidly once oil has been added to them; therefore, this salad should never be prepared in advance.

SERVES 4

A properly baked tomato, bubbling with fragrant melted cheese and herbs, is one of the most delightful ways to begin a meal, especially when the cheese is a good, sharp, aged cheddar from Herkimer County in upper New York State.

◆§ HERKIMER COUNTY ৪◆
BAKED TOMATOES

4 large, fresh tomatoes, not too soft
Salt and pepper to taste
French thyme
Grated cheese, parmesan or romano

½ lb. Herkimer County aged cheddar cheese, or other good, aged cheddar
2 Tbs. melted butter or margarine

Slice the tomatoes in half, against the core. Remove seeds and some of the meaty pulp, forming a pocket in each half. Salt and pepper each cavity and sprinkle liberally with French thyme and grated cheese. Cut cheddar cheese into small wedges or cubes, and stuff each half liberally. Drizzle a small amount of melted butter or margarine over each. Arrange on buttered baking dish, and bake in preheated oven at 350°F.

for 35 minutes, until tomato is tender but still retaining its shape and cheese is golden brown.

SERVES 4 TO 8

Long before the electric refrigerator and even the old-fashioned ice-box became a standard part of the kitchen, man had to eat his food almost as soon as he had cooked it. Gradually he managed to find the means to cook his food and eat it later. He used preservatives such as sugar, vinegar, and salt to prepare these dishes. One interesting dish created by Sicilian chefs solved the spoilage problem and preserved in the hot Sicilian climate, at least for a short time, a savory eggplant appetizer.

⋐ EGGPLANT CAPONATINA ⋑

1 large eggplant
¼ cup olive oil
2 cloves garlic
2 onions
1 cup celery, cut into small
  pieces
2 Tbs. tomato paste

¾ cup warm water
2 Tbs. capers
¼ cup green olives
3 Tbs. red wine vinegar
1½ Tbs. sugar
Salt and pepper

Peel the eggplant and cut into 1-inch slices. Put in a deep bowl and cover with brine (¼ cup of salt to 1 quart water). Place a plate or other large flat object over top of bowl to keep eggplant submerged in brine. Let stand for 2 hours in refrigerator. Drain and rinse each slice well. Dry slices between paper towels and cut into large cubes, about 1-inch square.

While eggplant is soaking, prepare the other ingredients. Mince the garlic very fine. Slice onions lengthwise, quite thin. Combine garlic, onion, and celery in a small bowl. In a glass, mix tomato paste with ¾ cup warm water, and stir until well blended. Rinse capers with cold water and set aside in strainer to drain well. Slice olives in halves.

Heat the olive oil in a large skillet, a cast-iron or other heavy one. Sauté eggplant cubes for several minutes. Remove the cubes from the pan with a slotted spoon and set aside in a bowl. Sauté garlic, onions, and celery in the same oil until onions are soft and translucent. Add tomato paste and water mixture, and continue to cook until celery is tender. Return eggplant to skillet, and add capers and olives. Heat vinegar and sugar in small saucepan until sugar is dissolved. Pour vinegar and dissolved sugar over eggplant mixture. Add salt and pepper to taste, and stir until all ingredients are well mixed. Simmer, covered, for 15 to 20 minutes, stirring 3 or 4 times to prevent sticking or burning. A little more water may be added if necessary. Serve hot or cold. This salad will keep well for about 1 week in your refrigerator.

SERVES 6 TO 8

The fragrant mushroom so highly prized in Italian cooking is prepared in every way imaginable. The Neapolitans, who have done more to adapt the love apple to their cookery than almost any other regional group in Italy, have produced a very special hot appetizer made with mushrooms in a tomato sauce seasoned with parsley, garlic, oregano, and black pepper. Neapolitans love to have their food livened with a little bit of *forte*, or strength, as they term it, and often freely season this dish with fiery hot crushed red pepper. A tasty dish, no matter how hot or mild, when eaten with crusty slices of Italian bread.

◆§ SPICED NEAPOLITAN MUSHROOMS §◆

1 lb. large fresh mushrooms
¼ cup olive oil
3 cloves garlic, finely minced
1 large tomato
2 Tbs. fresh parsley, finely chopped

½ tsp. oregano
Salt and pepper
½ tsp. crushed red pepper (optional)

Clean and slice the mushrooms into hammer shapes. Heat the oil in a heavy skillet and sauté the garlic and mushrooms for 5 minutes. Wash and slice the tomato into thin wedges. Add to the mushrooms along with the parsley and oregano. Salt and pepper to taste and, if desired, add the red pepper. Use the black pepper freely to impart a piquant taste to the dish. Cook an additional 10 minutes, stirring occasionally. Remove the mushrooms from the flame and hold for 10 minutes before serving.

SERVES 4

Shrimps, warm and swimming in a spiced tomato sauce, make a hunger-appeasing hot hors d'oeuvre which provides a very welcome change from the more conventional cold shrimp cocktail. Serve this appetizer with bread rusks or toasted biscuits to provide a continental touch.

⋪ HOT SPICED SHRIMP ঈ

½ lb. shrimp, about 20 me-
  dium-sized
1 clove garlic, finely minced
4 Tbs. green pepper, minced
2 Tbs. celery, finely minced

2 Tbs. olive oil
2 soft, ripe tomatoes,
  chopped
½ tsp. oregano
Salt and pepper

Clean and devein the shrimp. Sauté the garlic, green pepper, and celery in the oil over a low flame until lightly browned. Add the tomatoes and simmer gently for 20 minutes, until the consistency of a sauce. Strain the sauce through a coarse sieve and return to a saucepan. Add the shrimp and the seasonings. Simmer covered for 10 minutes. Remove from the heat and set aside for 5 additional minutes.

SERVES 4

Potato salad is a perennial favorite as the mainstay of barbecues, picnics, and cold summer suppers. Yet tomatoes are rarely associated with potatoes in salad. The old familiar potato salad uses, with some variations, simply potatoes, mayonnaise, and seasonings. Europeans have long made a potato salad which uses potatoes as a base but add many flavorful supplementary ingredients such as tomatoes, peppers, and anchovies. For this type of potato salad use oil rather than mayonnaise, an advantage when it comes to picnicking on a hot summer day when there is no ice to keep the mayonnaise from spoiling.

✌§ HUGO'S POTATO SALAD §✍

1 lb. potatoes
2 firm ripe tomatoes
1 small onion
10 pitted black olives, cut in halves
1 small roasted pepper, slivered, or 1 2-oz. jar slivered pimientoes

5 flat anchovy fillets
5 Tbs. olive oil
Salt and pepper
1 sprig fresh basil, chopped

Cook the potatoes, with their skins on, in boiling, salted water. When tender, drain and cool. Peel and cut the potatoes into rounds. Slice the tomatoes into wedges and put into a large bowl. Add the onion, olives, and pepper. Break the anchovies into small pieces and add to the salad. Toss gently, then add the potato slices, oil, salt, and pepper. Mix all gently and garnish with the basil. Chill before serving.

SERVES 4

Hearty, thin-sliced German rye bread is a great way to set off a crisp, cold, freshly cut plum tomato, particularly at cocktail time when a savory sardine spread covers the tomato. This easily prepared open-faced sandwich can serve equally well at tea-time or even for a small garden party, especially during balmy spells in early September when the plums are finding their way garden-fresh into markets all over the nation.

⌘ COCKTAIL PLUM SANDWICHES ⌘

1 can boneless and skinless
  sardines in oil
2 anchovy fillets
1 tsp. capers, rinsed and
  drained
1 tsp. minced onion
2 Tbs. mayonnaise

1 tsp. fresh lemon juice
1 tsp. finely minced parsley
Black pepper to taste
4 firm ripe plum tomatoes
4 slices German rye bread,
  or other thin-sliced dark
  bread

Combine the sardines, anchovy fillets, capers, onion, mayonnaise, lemon juice, parsley, and black pepper in a small bowl. Mash all together and blend thoroughly.

Slice the tomatoes into rounds, 4 per tomato.

Trim the crust from the bread and cut each slice into four squares. On each bread square place a tomato slice. On each tomato slice spread a liberal amount of the sardine mixture. Arrange on a serving platter.

SERVES 4

III

Soups

The first Europeans to make use of the culinary properties of the tomato were lordly gentlemen botanists who during the high Renaissance and up to the end of the 18th century kept extensive private gardens in which they collected curious shrubs, herbs, and plants. Strange herbs which came from the Americas particularly interested these patrician planters.

Not only did they grow rare plants but, inspired by their inquiring palates, they tasted the fruits of their gardens. These gentlemen botanists were the first Europeans to eat the tomato, raw and cooked.

In England these botanists were called "florists," a word which now is used for flower venders. The word lost its exclusive qualities as working-class Englishmen started raising flowers and herbs. The more aristocratic florists stopped breeding new plants and became collectors of rare, strange, and unusual shrubbery from all over the world.

One of the more noted 18th-century English horticulturists was Phillip Miller. He was a friend of Carolus Linnaeus, the Swedish botanist, who often visited Miller's gardens. Miller wrote extensively on the science of botany. As more and more plants of the New World were introduced into English gardens he made special comment on them. In his *Gardener's Dictionary*, written in 1752, he had this to say about the English use of tomatoes:

"The Italians and Spaniards eat these apples [tomatoes] as we do cucumbers with pepper, oil, and salt, and some eat them in sauces, etc., and in Soups they are now much used in England, especially this Sort which is preferred to all the other. This fruit gives an agreeable Acid to the Soup; though there are some persons who think them unwholesome from their great Moisture and Coldness."

Many scholars feel that this early botanical allusion to tomatoes as being "cold" is the origin of the fable that the tomato is poisonous. Early herbalists thought that any fruit considered "cold" was unfit to eat. Besides being thought of as "cold," the tomato, soon after it was brought to Europe in the 16th century, was placed by the Italian botanist Mattioli in the same family as the poisonous deadly nightshade, belladonna, henbane and mandrake.

After salad, soup was probably another important culinary milestone in the history of the tomato. "If the love apple is so good in salads, how might it taste in soups?" we can almost hear a 16th-century cook saying.

The soups prepared in those adventuresome tomato-cooking times were not the same sort of watery broths which are so common today. From the Middle Ages until the beginning of the 18th century, soups reflected the lusty, vigorous appetites of the hardy folk who ate them. These soups were crude, thick, chowdery substances which produced an inconsequential amount of thick, gravy-like liquid.

Many of these soups are still popular today. One of the most ancient of Neapolitan Minestre (thick, soup-like stews) is a tasty tomato pepper pot. This exquisite use of the tomato might well have been described by the English florist, John

Gerarde, when in 1597 he spoke of an Italian dish which was made with peppers, tomatoes, and oils.

⊌§ CIANFOTTA §∾

(Neapolitan pepper pot)

15 *ripe plum tomatoes*
2 *large potatoes*
¼ *cup olive oil*
1 *stalk celery, coarsely chopped*

2 *large onions, slivered lengthwise*
Salt and pepper
8 *Italian peppers*
1 *cup sliced zucchini squash*
4 *large fresh basil leaves*

Wash the tomatoes and pass them through a coarse sieve. Peel the potatoes and cut into round slices. Heat the oil in a heavy saucepan, and add onions and celery, cooking them until they become translucent and softened. Add tomatoes and bring to a boil. Add potatoes, and salt and pepper to taste. Cook about 10 minutes or until potatoes are half done. Add water, if necessary, to prevent burning and to maintain consistency of a soup-like broth. Add peppers, which have been seeded and sliced in quarters. Add squash. Put in the basil leaves and continue to cook over a moderate flame until the potatoes are tender. Allow to rest for a few minutes, then serve.

SERVES 4

Still a jet-age favorite despite its ancient background, chowder is often used as an all-in-one lunch or main supper dish. Chowder stems from an old French word, *chaudière*, the name for a vessel or pot used to heat foods or other materials. Chowders are soupy vegetable or fish dishes, often using milk for the liquid. Clam chowder is a typically American dish, combining clams, vegetables, and various herbs.

⊷ TOMATO MEATBALL CHOWDER ⊱

6 cups beef broth
6 cups fresh tomatoes,
  peeled and diced
2 tsp. sugar
2 tsp. salt
¼ tsp. ground black pepper
1 small clove garlic, finely
  chopped
2 cups mashed potatoes
2 cups fresh carrots, sliced
1 cup fresh potatoes, diced

1 cup fresh celery, diced
½ cup fresh mushrooms,
  sliced
1 Tbs. fresh parsley, finely
  chopped
¼ tsp. thyme leaves
¼ tsp. basil leaves
½ lb. ground meat
¼ tsp. salt
Dash ground black pepper
I Tbs. butter or margarine

Place the beef broth, tomatoes, sugar, salt, pepper, and garlic
in saucepan. Cover and cook for 15 minutes. Add mashed
potatoes, and continue cooking 10 minutes more until the soup
is thick. Add carrots, potatoes, celery, mushrooms, parsley,
thyme, and basil, and cook until vegetables are tender. Mix
meat with salt and pepper. Shape into ½ inch balls. Sauté in
butter until browned. Add to chowder.

MAKES 3 QUARTS

    Grandma Roth had her own special way with a "reputa-
tion" clam chowder that called for corn, fresh herbs, and lots
of tomatoes. Another of her favorite shellfish soups was one
which she called "Philadelphia Clam Chowder." In this version you can use canned clams.

⊷ GRANDMA ROTH'S WESTHAMPTON ⊱
CLAM CHOWDER

2 oz. diced salt pork
1 cup diced carrots
1 cup diced celery
1 cup chopped onion
1 cup diced potatoes

1 cup cut corn
½ tsp. thyme
3 sprigs fresh marjoram
Leaves from 2 small sprigs
  fresh rosemary

1 quart tomatoes, chopped
1½ dozen chowder clams, cleaned, chopped
2 cups strained clam broth

2 Tbs. chopped fresh parsley
Salt and pepper

In a large kettle sauté the salt pork until it is browned. Add 1 quart of water, carrots, celery, and onion, and cook for 10 minutes. Then add potatoes and tomatoes. Cook for an additional 10 minutes. Add chopped clams, clam broth, corn, thyme, marjoram, rosemary, parsley, and salt and pepper to taste. Simmer gently for 10 minutes.

MAKES 1 GALLON

Note: Grandma used to make this chowder in large quantities when fresh vegetables were in season because it lent itself easily to canning. It freezes equally as well.

⊷§ PHILADELPHIA CLAM CHOWDER §⊷

1-inch cube salt pork, diced
1 cup clam liquor
1 cup fish broth (obtained by boiling 1½ cups water with ½ lb. fish bones and heads for 25 minutes over low heat. Strain.)
½ cup sliced onions
1 cup diced potatoes

½ cup canned clams (or equal amount fresh, scalded clams)
1 cup fresh tomatoes, chopped
1 cup tomato juice
½ tsp. fresh thyme, chopped fine
Salt and pepper
Fresh parsley for garnish

In a large saucepan sauté salt pork until lightly browned. Add the clam liquor and fish broth, and bring to a boil. Skim off foam, then add onions and potatoes. Simmer for 15 minutes. Add clams, tomatoes, tomato juice, thyme, and salt and pepper to taste. Bring to boiling point, reduce heat, and simmer for 5 minutes. Serve with garnish of chopped parsley.

SERVES 4

Mediterranean tomato and shellfish lovers have a clam soup all their own. They use cockles, a type of clam peculiar to that part of the world. Here in the United States we use the versatile littleneck clam, a delicious New World shellfish.

⊷§ MEDITERRANEAN CLAM SOUP §⊶

2½ lbs. littleneck clams
6 sprigs fresh parsley
2 cloves garlic
2 Tbs. olive oil

2 Tbs. tomato paste, diluted
in 1 cup water
Salt and pepper
4 hard Italian biscuits or 2
split, toasted hard rolls

Discard any clams which have opened. Wash the rest thoroughly with a stiff brush to remove algae and sand. Wash the parsley, and chop it fine. Put half of it into a mortar with ½ of a garlic clove. Pound them together to form a paste.

In a saucepan sauté the remaining 1½ cloves garlic in oil until golden. Add the garlic-parsley paste, and cook for 15 seconds. Add the tomato paste in water, the clams, and pepper to taste. Cook covered for 5 minutes, until the shells are all open. Taste the broth, and add salt if needed. Garnish with the rest of the parsley, and serve over the biscuits or rolls.

SERVES 4

To the French, cream of tomato soup once spelled late summer, but we use canned tomatoes, which now retain true tomato flavor, to make this easy-to-prepare soup all year.

⊷§ POTAGE CRÊME DE TOMATES §⊶

¼ cup chopped onion
2 Tbs. butter or margarine
3½ cups canned tomatoes
3 Tbs. butter, melted

3 Tbs. flour
½ tsp. thyme
Salt and pepper
2½ cups light cream

Sauté the onion slowly in 2 tbs. butter until translucent. Pass the tomatoes and cooked onion through a fine sieve or food mill. In a saucepan, blend 3 tbs. butter with flour. Add the tomato-onion mixture, thyme, salt and pepper to taste. Simmer over a medium heat until thickened, being sure to stir constantly with a wire whisk. In a second saucepan, scald the cream. While the cream is still very hot, add the hot tomato mixture very slowly, stirring constantly, rapidly. Serve at once.

SERVES 6

Note: If the soup curdles, blend it with an electric mixer on high speed for a few minutes. This will give it a smoother texture.

Americans once knew that harvest time was the season to enjoy the very best of tomatoes. In this recipe two late summer treats are blended with noteworthy results. This soup can also be made satisfactorily with canned ingredients. This hearty dish can be listed among the classic creamed soups. The unusual addition of corn not only adds a firmer texture to the potage but hints of Creole origins as well.

◄§ GOLDEN HARVEST SOUP §►

2 cups cooked corn, canned
  or fresh
2 cups tomato purée
2 cups Velouté sauce*
  (p. 32)

Salt and pepper to taste
Fresh chopped chervil for
  garnish

Grind the corn, then pass it through a fine sieve. Combine the resultant purée with the tomato purée and Velouté sauce in a large saucepan. Salt and pepper to taste. Simmer over low heat for 15 minutes. Stir occasionally. Serve with chervil garnish.

SERVES 6

* VELOUTÉ SAUCE

2½ cups chicken broth
1 Tbs. chopped parsley
2 Tbs. chopped carrot
2 Tbs. chopped onion
1 large leaf basil

¼ tsp. sugar
Salt and pepper
1½ Tbs. flour
1½ Tbs. melted butter

In a saucepan combine the broth, parsley, carrot, onion, basil, sugar, salt, and pepper to taste. Simmer gently for 20 minutes. Strain through a hair sieve or cheesecloth. To this clear liquid add a roux made by blending flour with butter until smooth. Put over a low heat and bring to a boil, stirring constantly with a whisk. Continue boiling for 5 minutes, skimming and stirring. The sauce is now ready for use.

Ordinary tomato soup can be transformed into an epicurean potage by using some Continental touches. Proper choice of the herbs, a judicious addition of bouillon, and a dash of aged cheese can create a masterful first course that is certain to be well received and called on in future for encores.

⋖§ FRESH TOMATO SOUP §⋗

5 large tomatoes
3 basil leaves
¼ cup minced celery
1 small onion, minced
3 Tbs. olive oil
1 beef bouillon cube

¾ cup raw rice
½ tsp. sugar
Salt to taste
3 Tbs. grated cheese
3 Tbs. butter

Peel the tomatoes, and remove the cores. Wash the basil and chop fine. In a saucepan sauté basil, celery, and onion in olive oil until basil is wilted. Add the tomatoes and 2 quarts of water. Cover and simmer for 45 minutes. Add bouillon cube, rice, sugar, and salt to taste. Cover and simmer for 15 minutes, until rice is cooked. Add the cheese and butter, stir once and serve with additional cheese if desired.

SERVES 6

In Spain the word *gazpacho* refers to a cold, garlicky tomato soup. The origin of the word is lost, but many experts feel that this delicious soup was so named because of the sound of the mortar and pestle while the dish was being prepared.

⋐§ ANDALUSIAN GAZPACHO §⋑

5 *large ripe tomatoes, peeled and seeded*	1 *slice stale Italian bread*
	⅓ *cup olive oil*
6 *small green peppers, peeled and seeded*	¼ *cup wine vinegar*
	Salt
2 *cloves garlic*	*Croutons*

In an electric blender, purée the tomatoes, peppers, and garlic. Soak the slice of bread in water until it will absorb no more. Remove and drain it. Add this to the blender, and mix thoroughly with the tomato mixture. Put mixture in a bowl and chill for 3–4 hours. Then add the oil, vinegar, and 1½ cups water. Salt to taste. Cover the bowl and refrigerate for 4–5 hours more. When ready to serve, pour into bowls and top with croutons. At this time an ice cube may be added to each bowl to keep the soup as chilled as possible.

SERVES 4

In New Orleans the tomato is king of the soup pot. Many marvelous thick soups were created there for sharp epicurean palates. "Gumbo" is the Indian word for okra, and the thick soups in which okra is added are called "gumbos." These Creole soups are often complicated to prepare but are well worth the effort.

⇜ CRAB GUMBO ⇝

¼ cup raw rice
1 cup cooked crab meat
1 Tbs. butter or margarine
⅛ tsp. nutmeg
1 quart chicken broth
2 Tbs. butter
2 Tbs. flour
¼ cup okra

2 Tbs. sweet red pepper,
    chopped
2 large tomatoes, sliced and
    peeled
½ tsp. thyme
¼ tsp. marjoram
Pinch crushed red pepper
1 tsp. lemon juice

Boil the rice according to package directions. When the rice has been cooked, drain and rinse with cold water. Pass the rice and ½ cup of the crab meat through a fine sieve. Add 1 tbs. butter and the nutmeg.

In a saucepan heat the stock in which a roux of 2 tbs. butter and 2 tbs. flour has been blended. Bring to boil, stirring with a wire whisk. Simmer until broth thickens slightly, and skim off any foam. Add the crab-rice purée, okra, sweet pepper, slices of tomato, thyme, marjoram, crushed red pepper, and lemon juice. Simmer slowly for an hour. When ready to serve, put 2 tbs. of the remaining crab meat in each bowl and spoon the soup over it.

SERVES 4

⇜ CHICKEN SOUP CREOLE ⇝

2 whole chicken breasts,
    skinned, boned, cubed
4 large shallots, minced
3 Tbs. olive oil
2 Tbs. flour
1½ quarts chicken broth
2 Tbs. shredded country
    ham
½ cup green pepper,
    chopped

1½ cups fresh or canned to-
    matoes, peeled and
    chopped
½ cup raw rice
1 tsp. dry parsley
½ tsp. sweet marjoram
½ tsp. savory
¼ tsp. thyme
2 tsp. dry celery leaves
Dash black pepper

Sauté the chicken cubes and shallots in the oil until both are lightly browned. Stir in the flour until well blended. Add the broth. Bring mixture quickly to a boil, stirring constantly. Skim off any foam. Add the ham and green peppers. Cover tightly and simmer for 30 minutes. Add the tomatoes, rice, parsley, marjoram, savory, thyme, celery leaves, and black pepper. Simmer, covered, until the rice is tender. Stir occasionally to prevent burning. If the soup is too thick, add more broth or water to suit your taste.

SERVES 6

The love apple's agreeability as a table food is one of the vegetable's main charms. As the good Philip Miller noted, the delightful bit of acid imparted by the fruit adds a very pleasant piquancy to ordinary kitchen soups. This economy dish uses the carcass of a boned chicken, giblets, and wings. It is probably the least expensive soup made. Some extravagant people use an entire fryer or broiler to make this soup, but the idea of creating a masterful soup from otherwise unusable chicken parts is particularly pleasing to me. The soup should be prepared as soon as the chicken flesh is removed from the bones because the carcass does not keep well. The noodles are added the day the soup is served.

⋞§ MY FAVORITE CHICKEN SOUP §⋟

Giblets, wings, boned carcass, and tail from large chicken, or
1 small frying chicken with giblets
1 large celery stalk with leaves

1 large onion
3 sprigs parsley
3 fresh chopped seeded tomatoes
Salt and pepper to taste
1 tsp. dry marjoram
½ lb. fine egg noodles

Place in a large soup pot 2½ quarts of cold water and the chicken. Bring to a boil and skim. Chop the celery fine. Slice the onion into lengthwise strips. Mince the parsley. Add the celery, onion, parsley, tomatoes, salt, pepper, and the marjoram. Cover and simmer gently for 2 hours. Strain the hot broth through a fine sieve or several layers of cheesecloth to remove all solid particles. Return the broth to the kettle and bring to a boil. Add the noodles and a little additional salt and boil until the noodles are tender. Serve this soup with grated cheese if desired.

SERVES 4

When the magic of autumn begins to change the shop-worn greenery of summer into the precious golden hues of the harvest season, the time has come for making a good vegetable soup. Along the beautiful Ohio countryside farmers begin gathering in the fruits of their summer's labor in the field and have the freshest of ingredients for this dish. This hearty soup was a late autumn treat that was highly popular in 19th-century America and autumn was the only season when people could savor the full flavor of farm produce. Fortunately all the ingredients for this soup can now be obtained the year round. The proportions of vegetables can be altered to suit your own taste.

⇜ OHIO VEGETABLE SOUP ⇝

2 large knuckle or marrow bones, split
1 large onion
1 yellow turnip
3 potatoes

12 medium tomatoes
2 cups shredded cabbage
3 large sprigs parsley
¼ cup celery leaves
Salt and pepper

Put the bones in a large soup kettle and cover with cold water. Bring to a boil and skim. Cover tightly and let simmer over low heat for 3 hours. Add more water if necessary to keep bones completely covered. Strain the stock through a fine sieve or several layers of cheesecloth and discard the bones. Return stock to the kettle.

Slice the onion lengthwise into thin strips. Peel the turnip and dice. Peel and dice the potatoes. Add the onion, turnip, and potatoes to the stock and simmer over low flame for ½ hour. While the soup simmers, scald the tomatoes in boiling water for 15–20 seconds, cool under running water, and peel. Quarter and seed the tomatoes over a strainer, so that the juice will collect in a small bowl placed underneath. Add the tomatoes, cabbage, parsley, celery leaves, and salt and pepper to taste. Simmer, covered, for an additional 1 hour, stirring occasionally and adding more water if necessary to keep vegetables covered.

SERVES 8

IV

Fish Dishes

L ittle do lovers of exquisitely prepared seafood realize how very much they owe to the good priest Hieronymus Cardon, who accompanied Hernando Cortés on his conquest of Mexico. The strange seeds which he sent to his brother in Cadiz produced lush, ripe tomatoes that eventually enhanced fish cookery throughout the world.

There are people who dispute the fact that Cardon introduced the tomato to Europe because he was supposed to have been a Jesuit, and that religious order was not founded until 1539, many years after the subjugation of Mexico by the Spaniards. Nevertheless, some members of Cortés's entourage did encounter the tomato among the beautiful gardens of the Aztecs and brought it back to Europe. Perhaps, for lack of a known hero, claim for the tomato's discovery should rest with the redoubtable warrior himself, Cortés.

Fish takes as readily to sauce as it does to water. The prime reason for this adaptability is that properly prepared sauces tend to "de-fish" or mask a strong fish taste. The tomato's tangy flavor not only mutes any overpowering fishy taste but blends and enlivens delicate fish tones. Any fish platter is thus made more delectable against the superb background of the tomato.

Aside from its delightful taste, the love apple's warm, vividly red color is another reason for its popularity in fish cookery. The pastel shades of fish flesh are set off against a ruddy tint, and an artistically gratifying as well as a tasty work of art is created.

The culinary use of the tomato is nowhere more evident than in the *meridionale,* or southern, branch of Italian cookery. Among the divers southern Italian styles of cooking, the cuisine of Naples is outstanding in its use of the tomato.

What is termed "Neapolitan cooking" in the United States usually encompasses the entire range of the broad Italian Campagnia. Each small province in this area adds its own delightful nuance to the Neapolitan repertoire. One would be hard put to find seafood more carefully and lovingly prepared with tomatoes than the dishes served along that part of the Campagnia called the Amalfi Coast.

Amalfi itself was once one of the four maritime republics of Italy. Early in its history as a trading city a great earthquake occurred, and almost all of Amalfi went sliding into the sea—a commercial catastrophe from which the town has not yet recovered. This disaster left the area as one of the most breathtakingly beautiful in all Italy. It also turned the local inhabitants to the pursuits of more immediate delights, such as the preparation of their delicious native seafood.

Amalfitani have gone to the four corners of the world spreading their savory cuisine before appreciative diners. Their descendants have grown in numbers, particularly in the United States and especially in New York City, where my cousin Jim Toriello and I live.

Jim's restaurant, the Amalfi, is probably the best Neapolitan restaurant of its type in the city. One of the reasons for this preeminence is the scrupulous care taken in the purchase and preparation of the foods served there. So great is the Amalfi's reputation that *Life* magazine has printed Jim's minestrone recipe in its "Great Dinner's" series.

At the Amalfi they have a special touch with seafood, and among the restaurant's dazzling list of seafood dishes I have chosen two which make delicious use of the tomato. These dishes have been adapted to the seafood which is freshly caught along the Atlantic coast of the United States.

A dish to my particular liking is one of Jim's specialties, Fresh Maine Lobster, Fra Diavolo. Many people say that this dish was named after a famous Neapolitan bandit who was called "Friar Devil," *Fra Diavolo* to his fellow countrymen. *Fra Diavolo* had a true Neapolitan love of tomato sauce, but also like a true Neapolitan, he preferred his food extremely piquant.

◄§ FRESH MAINE LOBSTER ξ► FRA DIAVOLO

2 1½-lb. live lobsters
1 onion, coarsely minced
1 clove garlic, coarsely minced
3 Tbs. light olive oil
1 1-lb., 12 oz. can peeled plum tomatoes

Salt and pepper
½ tsp. crushed red pepper (or less if desired)
3 Tbs. chopped Italian parsley

Have your fish dealer kill and cut up the lobsters. If you prefer to do this chore yourself, put each live lobster on its back, and cut between tail shell and body. Then slice the lobster lengthwise. Twist claws off, and crack them so the meat can be easily removed. Lift the stomach (which is the small sac between the eyes) gently out of the split lobster. If the intestinal vein does not come out with the stomach, lift it out with your fingers or a fork. Cut up the lobsters so that you have 12 pieces, including the claws.

Brown lobster, onion, and garlic in hot oil in a large cast-iron skillet. When they are just lightly browned, add the tomatoes and mix. Salt and pepper to taste. At this moment add as much red pepper as your constitution can stand. Be cautious because ½ tsp. is considered a formidable amount. Cover the lobster and simmer no longer than 15 minutes. When the sauce begins to thicken it is ready to serve. Just before removing the lobster from the flame, add chopped parsley and stir. Remove the lobster to a warmed serving dish, and pour the sauce over and around it.

SERVES 2

Along the Amalfi coast most fishermen and sailors are gourmets. They love good food and will settle for nothing but the best. These seamen, due to the nature of their work, are often far removed from proper stoves and shoreside kitchens. They have to make do the best they can, and so well have they improvised that they have created an entire branch of Italian cooking. It is known as *alla marinara* or sailor's-style. Seamen all over Italy have added to this genre of cooking, but the most widely known is the Neapolitan method, in which food is cooked in a richly seasoned tomato sauce.

The Neapolitan sailors used tiny plum tomatoes in their cooking, chopped them fine without peeling (which is an improvement, however), and quickly cooked the sauce. In this swiftness of preparation lies the secret of the sailors' touch, resulting in incomparable dishes with all the verve of fresh tomato taste. The same method may be used with canned plum tomatoes to create a magnificent dish without the trouble of peeling the tomatoes.

Jim Toriello is most partial to a fresh filet of sole or flounder cooked so that it is redolent with the full flavor of the sea. It is a most beautiful sight bubbling in its rich tomato sauce. This recipe is an ancient one first created by food-wise Neapolitan fishermen.

◄§ FILLET OF SOLE ALLA MARINARA §►

1 medium onion, minced
1 or 2 garlic cloves, minced
2 Tbs. light olive oil
1 1-lb., 12 oz. can peeled plum tomatoes

1 tsp. oregano
Salt and pepper
8 large fillets of sole
2 Tbs. chopped Italian parsley

In your largest skillet, sauté the onion and garlic in hot oil until golden brown. Add the tomatoes, oregano, salt and pepper to taste. Simmer, uncovered, for 15 minutes. Carefully add the fillets, spooning enough sauce over them to cover. Simmer, covered, for 10 minutes. Add chopped parsley 1 minute before removing from flame. Transfer the fillets to heated platter. Spoon sauce over and around the fish.

SERVES 4 TO 6

Shrimp, one of America's favorite seafoods, is also its most versatile, especially when paired with the equally versatile tomato. Shrimp and tomato suppers are also easy to prepare, particularly when frozen, peeled, deveined shrimp are used.

◄§ FRENCH-FRIED SHRIMP WITH §► TOMATO-WINE SAUCE

1½ cups chili sauce
½ cup tomato juice
½ tsp. Worcestershire sauce
1 dash Tabasco sauce
½ tsp. chili powder
1 garlic clove

¼ cup dry white wine
1 Tbs. lemon juice
1 bay leaf
1 clove
2 (10-oz.) packages frozen breaded shrimp

Combine sauce ingredients in a jar. Cover and let stand several hours. Strain and serve with French-fried shrimp, using frozen breaded shrimp according to package directions.

SERVES 6 TO 8

Garlic and tomatoes are as beloved in Marseilles as they are in Naples; witness this difficult yet delicious luncheon pie.

⋘ COD PIE A LA MARSEILLES ⋙

6 *puff pastry shells, available frozen, ready to bake*
2 *lbs. drawn cod*
1 *tsp. salt*
1 *Tbs. onion, chopped*
1 *small whole carrot*
1 *Tbs. chopped parsley*
4 *peppercorns*
1 *small bay leaf*

2 *Tbs. flour*
1½ *Tbs. oil*
1 *cup tomato purée*
1 *garlic clove*
3 *Tbs. butter*
1 *dozen fresh oysters, cleaned and shucked*
Salt and white pepper

Bake the pastry shells according to package directions. Poach the drawn cod in 3 cups of water to which you have added the 1 tsp. salt, chopped onion, carrot, parsley, peppercorns, and bay leaf. Poach for 15–20 minutes or until fish easily flakes. Carefully remove fish from broth and set aside to cool for a few minutes. While it is cooling, strain the broth and put 1¼ cups of the liquid into a saucepan. Mix flour and oil until smooth, stir into the broth, and cook over a low heat, stirring constantly until thickened.

Flake the fish from the bones. Add tomato purée to the thickened fish broth, along with garlic. Cook 10 minutes over low heat, stirring several times. Remove garlic. Strain the sauce through a sieve and add butter. Stir well and to the sauce add flaked cod, raw oysters, and salt and white pepper to taste. Bring to a boil and allow to boil exactly 2 minutes. Remove from heat and spoon into pastry shells. Serve immediately.

SERVES 6

⊷ SHRIMP SALAD IN TOMATO ⊷
TOWERS

1 lb. shrimp, fresh or frozen, or 2 (8 oz.) packages peeled and deveined shrimp	*Salt and pepper*
	¼ cup diced green pepper
	⅓ cup cooked salad dressing
	6 large tomatoes
1½ cups cold cooked rice	*Chicory*
3 hard-cooked eggs, chopped	

Clean shrimp if necessary, and cook in enough boiling salted water to cover them for 3 to 5 minutes, or until shrimp are bright pink. Drain shrimp and chill. Reserve six whole shrimp for garnishing; dice remainder. Combine chopped shrimp with rice, hard-cooked eggs, salt and pepper to taste, and green pepper. Toss with salad dressing. Peel tomatoes if desired and cut crosswise into 3 slices. Sprinkle with salt. On a bed of chicory, reassemble each tomato, stem end down, spooning shrimp salad mixture between slices as you stack them. Top each tomato tower with a whole shrimp pegged with a toothpick.

SERVES 6

Another French dish, inspired by the famous Coquilles St. Jacques, can also be served in pastry shells as a tasty yet simple blend of scallops, tomatoes, mushrooms, and cream.

The coquilles are natural scallop shells (fireproof metal or porcelain shells are also used at times), used as containers for baking and browning various dishes. The legend of the coquilles is rather a romantic one linked with St. James of Compostela, or St. Jacques in French, a revered holy man.

One day a pagan bridegroom was riding recklessly along the shore and was tossed into the sea by his horse. Miraculously rescued by St. Jacques, he was converted to Christianity on the spot. Safe ashore, he found himself covered with scallop shells, which were believed to be a sign from St. Jacques and have thus become identified in French cooking with him.

◦§ TOMATOES ST. JACQUES §◦

1 qt. scallops
1 bottle (8-oz.) clam juice
½ cup water
½ tsp. salt
¼ tsp. ground black pepper
1 bay leaf
1 fresh onion, quartered
2 sprigs fresh parsley
4 Tbs. butter or margarine

½ lb. fresh mushrooms, sliced
3 ripe tomatoes, peeled and chopped
2 Tbs. butter or margarine
3 Tbs. flour
3 Tbs. heavy cream
½ to ¾ cup grated Parmesan cheese

Wash and drain scallops. Place in saucepan with clam juice, water, salt, pepper, bay leaf, onion, and parsley. Bring to boil and simmer gently for 6 minutes. Strain; reserve liquid. Discard onion, bay leaf, and parsley. Slice scallops. Sauté mushrooms and tomatoes in melted butter (4 tbs.) for 10 minutes, stirring frequently. Add scallops. In saucepan melt the 2 tbs. butter, stir in flour and cream, and cook until smooth. Stir in reserved scallop liquor. Cook, stirring constantly, until thickened. Combine with scallop, mushroom, and tomato mixture. Pour into 2 quart shallow baking dish. Sprinkle with cheese and broil at 500°F. for 6 to 8 minutes or until cheese has melted and browned. Serves 6 as main dish or 12 as appetizer baked in shells.

The festive color of the tomato lends itself ideally to the Yule season, especially when joined with as delicious a shellfish as the South African lobster.

⋖§ SOUTH AFRICAN ROCK LOBSTER §⋗ HOLIDAY STYLE

1 garlic clove, minced
1 Tbs. oil
1 6-oz. can tomato paste
1 6-oz. can water
1 1-lb. can whole tomatoes
⅛ tsp. crushed red pepper or cayenne
½ tsp. salt

⅛ tsp. pepper
½ tsp. basil
1 4-oz. can mushrooms and liquid
6 South African rock lobster tails, thawed
¼ cup oil

In heavy skillet, sauté garlic in 1 tbs. oil for a few minutes. Add tomato paste, can of water, tomatoes, red pepper, salt, pepper, and basil. Cook slowly for about an hour. Stir occasionally, and add a little more water if needed. Mixture should be very thick. Ten minutes before end of cooking time add mushrooms and liquid. Remove thawed tails from shells. Cut in large pieces. Brown tails in remaining hot oil, and add to sauce.

SERVES 6 TO 8

Everyone is familiar with the famous French bouillabaisse and the Italian cacciucco fish chowders, but the granddaddy of them all is the tasty Greek kakavia, or fisherman's stew, which has been made by Greek fishermen since Hector was a pup. The word *kakavia* is derived from *kakoira-kasorola*, which means "pot." *Bouillabaisse* comes from the French word *bouillotte*, which also means "pot." *Cacciucco* is so similar in sound to its Greek ancestor that it needs no etymylogical explanation.

The one great and lasting memory of all these fish stews is their uniquely delicious taste. Aside from their mutual seafood ancestry, this may be attributed to two classic ingredients: olive oil, used generously, and the fortunate addition of tomatoes.

⊷ GREEK FISHERMAN'S STEW ᵜ

2 medium onions, sliced
½ cup olive oil
1 lb. plum tomatoes, peeled
and chopped
1 lb. assorted small fish
(fresh sardines, butterfish,
snappers, smelts, young
flounder), drawn and left
whole

Salt and pepper to taste
1 large haddock fillet, cubed
1 large halibut fillet, cubed
⅓ lb. shelled, deveined
shrimp
3 rock lobster tails, shelled
and cut into pieces
4 to 6 hard biscuits

In a large soup pot sauté the onion slices in hot oil. Add the tomatoes and simmer 5 minutes. Add the small whole fish, salt and pepper, and water to cover. Simmer gently for 25 to 35 minutes. Pass all through a sieve, pressing the flesh of the fish through and discarding the bones. Return to soup pot. Add haddock, halibut, shrimp, and lobster tails. Add more water to cover. Simmer for 25 minutes. Serve over the hard biscuits in large soup bowls.

SERVES 4 TO 6

Fishermen the world over have a knack of preparing seafood in a plain yet appetizing manner. In the Latin countries of the Mediterranean they love their shellfish and squid almost as much as tomatoes. When they combine all three the results are an easy to prepare fisherman's "hot pot." If you haven't any shellfish handy, you can use the canned variety and bottled clam juice for sea essence. If frozen squid is not stocked in your local supermarket, use crabmeat. Fishermen are versatile fellows.

The sailor's hash below is a superb flaming-hot accompaniment to a seaside picnic or a Green Room dinner served in the open air. For American tastes the piquancy of the dish is best overcome with hearty draughts of beer or lemonade, although fishermen drink wine with the hash—often in quantity-to-quench the fiery taste.

⋖§ SAILOR'S HASH §⋗

2½ lbs. assorted shellfish
  (shrimp, scallops, clams,
  oysters, mussels)
1 lb. squid
3 Tbs. fresh parsley, very
  finely chopped
1 garlic clove
3 Tbs. olive oil

1 cup dry white wine
2¼ cups peeled, seeded and
  chopped tomatoes
¼ tsp. crushed red pepper
Salt and pepper
6 slices Italian bread
3 Tbs. olive oil

Clean the shellfish and squid. Mince the parsley and garlic. Cut squid into bite-size pieces. In an enamel fry pan, sauté squid in 3 tbs. hot oil for several minutes, turning often. Add the wine, and cook over high flame until evaporated. Add tomatoes, parsley, garlic, red pepper, salt, and pepper to taste. Cook, covered, over moderate heat for 20 minutes. While squid is cooking, steam shellfish in salted water until shells of the clams, scallops, oysters, and mussels are open and the shrimp have turned pink. Strain the liquor and reserve. Remove fish from shells and devein shrimp. A few minutes before the squid is done cooking, add shellfish and their liquor to fry pan.

While the mixture is cooking, fry the bread slices in hot oil. When slices are golden brown, transfer each to a shallow soup bowl. Spoon the fish and sauce over fried bread.

SERVES 6

The fireless cooker is a marvelous instrument which cooks by means of preheated stones. Phil Havens, of Westhampton Beach, Long Island, is the proud owner of one of these wonderful cookers, which never burns or scorches food. He is also an inveterate fisherman and has devised this special cod dish in which the subtle flavors of the tomato and French thyme mingle.

Phil Havens has geared his famous recipe for those lesser mortals not fortunate enough to own a fireless cooker.

✤ PHIL HAVEN'S CODFISH BAKE ✤

¼ cup oil
2 2-lb. cod, pan-dressed
2 large fresh tomatoes, cut
  in thick slices

½ tsp. powdered thyme
Salt and pepper

With half of the oil, cover the bottom of a large baking dish. Place the fish side by side in dish. Arrange the tomato slices over fish, sprinkle each with remaining oil, dust with thyme, and salt and pepper to taste. Bake in a preheated 350°F. oven for 20 minutes or until fish flakes easily.

SERVES 4

This simple recipe readily attests to how the tomato, when judiciously used in a skillet, can raise a sometimes dry fish steak into a juicy, mouthwatering main course fit for any gourmet's table.

✤ SKILLET STEAKS ✤

1 lb. can peeled plum toma-
  toes
1 small onion
2 Tbs. olive oil
3 leaves fresh basil

4 halibut steaks (about 3
  lbs.)
¼ cup olive oil
Salt and pepper
2 small leeks, chopped
¼ cup dry white wine

Chop the tomatoes coarsley. Chop the onion, and brown it in 2 tbs. oil. Add tomatoes and basil. Simmer, covered, for 20 minutes. Check the sauce a few times to make sure it has not thickened too much. Then put it through a food mill.

While sauce is cooking, wash and dry the fish steaks. Heat the ¼ cup oil in a large skillet. Salt and pepper the steaks and carefully arrange in pan. Add the chopped leeks, and fry until fish is browned on one side (for about 5 minutes).

Add the wine and cook over high heat until wine evaporates. Lower the flame, and turn the fish. Continue cooking for 5 minutes more; then pour the tomato sauce over the steaks. Cook 10 minutes longer, carefully turning the fish once. Let fish rest in pan off the flame for 10 minutes before serving.

SERVES 4

Swordfish St. Denis is a subtle blend of herbs, tomatoes, and strong red wine. Cooking this dish is a little tricky because of the long time the fish is over the heat. The secret lies in using a low flame and handling the steaks gently.

⇜§ SWORDFISH ST. DENIS §⇝

½ cup canned plum tomatoes, or 3 fresh plum tomatoes, peeled and chopped

1 large onion, sliced lengthwise

3 Tbs. oil

1 garlic clove, quartered

2 large swordfish steaks

2 tsp. chopped fresh basil

2 Tbs. fresh parsley, chopped coarsely

1 tsp. fresh thyme, minced fine

Salt and pepper

1 cup dry red wine

If canned tomatoes are used, chop coarsely. Brown onions in the hot oil. When nearly done, add the garlic for a few minutes. Put in the fish and cook over a very low flame for 5 minutes. Add the tomatoes, basil, parsley, thyme, salt and pepper to taste, and wine. Cook gently, uncovered, for 20 minutes, carefully turning the steaks once. When cooked, remove the fish to a warmed platter. Sieve the sauce, and pour it over the fish.

SERVES 4

The warm Mediterranean flavor of anchovies, dripping with the essences of the sea, is another tasty luncheon treat when combined with a tomato rarebit.

⊷§ TOMATO RAREBIT ON TOAST §⊶
WITH ANCHOVIES

3 large fresh tomatoes
2 Tbs. olive or salad oil
2 Tbs. fresh lemon juice
1 tsp. salt
⅛ tsp. ground black pepper

½ cup grated Cheddar
  cheese
2 Tbs. fine dry bread crumbs
¼ cup butter or margarine
6 rounds hot, buttered toast
Anchovies for garnish

Wash tomatoes, cut in half and place them, cut sides up, on a baking sheet. Sprinkle with olive oil, lemon juice, salt, and black pepper. Place under broiler for 5 minutes. Sprinkle with cheese and bread crumbs. Dot with butter or margarine. Place under broiler to brown, 2 to 3 minutes. Serve on rounds of hot, buttered toast. Garnish as desired with anchovies.

SERVES 6

The famed Middle East kebabs—skewered bits of marinated fish flesh—might take a long time to fully prepare but are the delights of clambakes or seaside cookouts. This recipe can be adapted to winter use in the kitchen.

⊷§ FISH KEBABS §⊶

3 Tbs. salad oil
2 Tbs. cider vinegar
¾ tsp. salt
¾ tsp. garlic salt
½ tsp. coarsely ground
  black pepper
½ tsp. onion salt

½ tsp. thyme leaves
1½ lbs. fish steaks, cut ¾-
  inch thick
Cherry tomatoes
Eggplant cubes
Frankfurter rolls

Combine oil, vinegar and seasonings. Cut fish into 1-inch squares and mix with marinade. Let stand overnight or for 4 to

5 hours. Just before cooking, place fish squares on skewers, alternating with tomatoes and parboiled eggplant squares. (To parboil eggplant, place in saucepan with 1 inch of boiling water and cook for about 2 or 3 minutes.) Place kebabs on broiler pan under broiler heat. Broil for 7 to 10 minutes or until fish is brown and flaky. Serve in split frankfurter rolls.

SERVES 6

V

Poultry and Meat Dishes

One of the many sad slanders whispered against the tomato is that our early American forebears were so frightened by the vegetable's poisonous reputation that they did not dare to eat it.

The truth, however, is that the tomato was known and enjoyed by many early colonists in both the Northern and Southern Hemisphere. North American settlers were perhaps not as aware of the tomato as were the Spaniards in Mexico, but by the start of the 18th century, particularly in Virginia, the tomato was a common garden vegetable. And why shouldn't it have been? The tomato was discovered by the first European colonists in Mexico, and word of the new tasty red berry undoubtedly spread to English and French colonies.

The tomato's fame fanned out from Latin colonies such as New Orleans and St. Augustine to the southern British colonies. It was an unheralded, quiet invasion, and the love apple went almost unnoticed, being as much a part of the strange New World diet as maize and squash. A reason for the tomato's popularity, particularly in Virginia, might have been the loyalty of that colony's inhabitants to the Crown.

Virginia remained true to the Stuart kings when Oliver Cromwell, Lord High Protector, set up the British Commonwealth and drove the Monarchists away. Cromwell was a particularly dour ruler and loved simple, plain fare on his table. Even at state functions his stomach despised the elaborate French dishes which were served. He refused to eat them, and they were placed at his table merely for ornamentation.

In France, the tomato enjoyed a reputation as a love token and Cromwell, proud Puritan that he was, shrank from the tomato, because of this reputation and because of the tomato's reputed aphrodisiac powers. His followers banned the foreign love apple from British tables, declaring it a sinful food, and thus closed the kitchen doors of the faithful from the delights of the tomato. Of course, loyal Virginians paid no attention to this attack on the tomato and nobly went on raising and eating the fruit.

Thomas Jefferson, a famous Virginian, was extremely fond of tomatoes and, in 1781, penned a few lines about how well the scarlet fruit was doing in his Monticello gardens. During his term as President of the United States, from 1801 to 1809, he made notes of the season when fresh tomatoes arrived at the produce stalls in Washington, D.C.

Many people feel that the northern colonies followed the Puritan pronouncement against the tomato and used the pretty plants simply as ornamental vines. The fruit, as an eatable product, thus remained unknown in these areas for many years. Still it seems hard to believe that the tomato remained absent from the dinner plates of the North for long. Lawmakers went to Washington from every state in the Union, and it seems perfectly plausible to conjecture that there ultimately were educated palates in the northern areas of the United States where the tomato was eaten with great relish.

Despite this theory it is apparent that most of the inhabitants of the Middle Atlantic and New England states were totally ignorant of the tomato's virtues as a table fruit. The first man daring enough to publically smash this ignorance was Colonel Robert Gibbon Johnson, who ate a "poisonous" love apple in 1820 on the courthouse steps of Salem, New Jersey. The astonished townspeople who witnessed this event expected Colonel Johnson to immediately drop to his doom. He survived, and kept on eating tomatoes. Since the juicy red tomato looked so good, some of the startled observers eventually followed the Colonel's example.

Two years after this momentous occurrence, the Grant Thorburn Company of New York, and other New England seed houses, listed the tomato as a nutritious vegetable. Soon, daring New Englanders began nibbling on the pretty, plump tomato, and by 1834 the fruit was being eaten in huge quantities by most Americans. Not only were the tomatoes eaten raw but they were used in recipes gleaned from Europeans and fellow countrymen in the South.

One of the first foods with which tomato was used by early Americans was meat. Game was plentiful in the United States during the 19th century, and at that time it constituted a major portion of the average diet. Since Americans retained the British habit of consuming large quantities of meat, the love apple was a welcome addition to baked, braised, and stewed meats.

Tomatoes not only added color and flavor to these meat dishes, but the acid content of the fruit helped break down the tough protein fibers of stringy game. Many early American dishes which used tomatoes were intriguing stews composed of small game, particularly squirrel or lean wild rabbit. Since small game has become a kitchen rarity for most of us, I have geared several of these old recipes to poultry.

A fine old Virginia dish is a delightful oven-baked stew which has not only the flavor of tomatoes but the wild country taste of slip-skin, or Concord-type, grape wine. These grapes are native to the United States and impart a more fragrant flavor to foods than do the drier European grape wines.

๔ร RICHMOND STEW ยั๛

2 3½-lb. stewing fowl, quartered
Salt and pepper
2 lbs. fresh tomatoes, peeled
  and sliced

1 large onion, chopped
2 sweet green peppers,
  seeded and chopped
4 Tbs. butter
1 cup Catawba wine

Place the fowl in the bottom of a large roasting pan. Salt and
pepper to taste. Cover with tomato slices, onion, and peppers
and dot evenly with butter. Pour over this 1 cup of Catawba
wine. Cover tightly and bake in a 325°F. oven for 3 hours or
until the fowl is tender and tomatoes form a sauce. Transfer
fowl to a heated serving dish and pour sauce over it.

SERVES 6

Another rich old Southern stew which resembles the one-
pot soup dinners of medieval times takes about 3½ hours just
for cooking, and consists of tomatoes, a tough small animal
such as squirrel or fowl, corn, and one small pod of dried
chili pepper. This latter touch hints of Mexican influence.

๔ร BROWN'S RICH HUNTING STEW ยั๛

2 slices bacon
1 small onion, minced fine
1 qt. tomatoes (4 cups),
  peeled and chopped
1 dried chili pepper

1 cut-up stewing fowl, or 2
  squirrels, cut up
¼ cup dried bread crumbs
½ cup cut corn, cooked
2 Tbs. mashed potatoes
Salt and pepper

Dice the bacon slices and fry in a large Dutch oven over low
heat until browned. Add the onion and brown well. Add the
tomatoes and simmer, covered, for 1 hour. Add the chili
pepper and fowl or squirrel, and stew, covered, for 2 more
hours. Add the bread crumbs, corn, potatoes, and salt and

pepper to taste. Cook, uncovered, for one-half hour. Put fowl in a large serving bowl and pour gravy over it.

SERVES 4

A stew which had its origins in mysterious, far-away India was brought here by Southern sea captains to delight their ladies, who promptly added just the right touch of tomato to enhance the dish's many fine attributes.

✑§ COUNTRY CAPTAIN ટ∾

1 *broiler-fryer chicken, cut
  in serving pieces*
1 *tsp salt*
Pepper
¼ *cup butter or margarine*
1 *medium onion, chopped*
1 *small green pepper,
  chopped*
1 *garlic clove, crushed*

2 *tsp. curry powder*
½ *tsp. leaf thyme*
1 *can (1 lb.) seasoned
  stewed tomatoes*
¼ *cup currants or raisins*
Hot cooked rice
Toasted blanched almonds
Chutney

Sprinkle chicken pieces on both sides with salt and pepper. Heat butter in large skillet. Add chicken and brown on all sides. Remove chicken from skillet and add onion, green pepper, garlic, curry powder, and thyme. Cook until onion is tender but not brown. Add stewed tomatoes, currants or raisins, and chicken. Cook, covered, for 20 to 30 minutes, until chicken is tender. Serve over rice with almonds and chutney.

SERVES 4

American hotel and saloon keepers of the 19th century reflected the magnificence of their gilded age of plenty by leaning heavily on preparing and serving foreign foods. Dishes hinting of their country of origin and glossed over with fancy French or other foreign touches were all the rage.

◄§ MEXICAN CHICKEN, SALOON STYLE ﴾►

1 frying chicken, cut in serving pieces
3 Tbs. olive oil
1 slice bacon
2 garlic cloves
1 small onion, sliced thin
1 cup tomato sauce
2 beef bouillon cubes dissolved in 1 cup water
1 Tbs. flour mixed thor-
oughly with 3 Tbs. cold
water
¼ tsp. powdered thyme

¼ tsp. powdered sage
½ tsp. marjoram
Salt and pepper to taste
1 small sweet red pepper,
finely minced
¾ cup peeled tomatoes,
seeded and chopped
½ cup home-made chili
sauce (see Chapter 7)
2 slices firm bread, cut into
tiny cubes
4 Tbs. butter or margarine

In a large skillet sauté the chicken pieces in the hot oil until browned on all sides. Remove from pan and set aside. In same oil brown the bacon, which has been cut into pieces, the garlic, and onion. Drain off excess oil. Add the tomato sauce, bouillon, and flour mixture. Stir well and simmer for a few minutes. Add thyme, sage, marjoram, salt and pepper, and sweet red pepper. Simmer for 35 minutes. Strain and put back in skillet. Add chicken, stir well and simmer 35 minutes, covered, or until the chicken is tender.

While mixture is simmering, stew the tomatoes until they are thick. This can be accomplished by boiling them in an uncovered saucepan over a high heat for 20 minutes or less. Stir often to prevent sticking. Add tomatoes to the chili sauce and blend the two well.

In a heavy frying pan, brown bread cubes in butter. Stir often to allow even cooking.

When chicken is cooked, remove to a serving dish and pour its sauce over it. Garnish with croutons and serve with tomato-chili mixture.

SERVES 4

The most beloved of all the familiar Southern hunting stews is the classic Brunswick stew, which makes use of a hearty base of tomatoes to form a magnificent, velvety gravy. It is also an economical dish because a modest amount of chicken can be stretched to satisfy six hearty appetites.

◄§ BRUNSWICK STEW ¿►

1 broiler-fryer chicken, cut in serving pieces
1 tsp. monosodium glutamate
3 tsp. salt, divided
4 Tbs. butter or margarine
2 medium onions, sliced
1 20-oz. can tomatoes
1 6-oz. can tomato paste
2 cups bouillon or consommé

1 cup finely diced celery with leaves
¼ tsp. each leaf marjoram and thyme
1 10-oz. package frozen whole kernel corn
1 10-oz. package frozen lima beans
2 Tbs. flour
3 Tbs. melted butter or margarine

Sprinkle chicken with monosodium glutamate and 1 tsp. of the salt. Melt butter in deep kettle. Brown chicken and remove. Add onions and brown lightly. Return chicken to kettle. Add tomatoes, tomato paste, bouillon or consommé, celery, herbs, and remaining 2 tsp. salt. Cover and simmer for about 1 hour. Add corn and lima beans, and cook for 20 minutes longer. Blend flour into melted butter. Add small amount of hot liquid from stew, stirring until smooth. Stir this mixture into stew, and cook for 2 minutes. Serve with hot corn bread.

SERVES 6

My wonderful sister-in-law, Evie St. Dennis, is one of the better cooks in Clinton, New York, and she has devised a marvelous chicken dish which is as versatile as her culinary background—English and Italian. There's no need to watch this pot, Evie says, "since a little over-cooking can't hurt."

❧ EVIE'S COMPANY CHICKEN ❧

1 *lb. Italian sweet sausage*	2 *Tbs. chopped parsley*
2 *Tbs. olive oil*	*Salt and pepper to taste*
6–8 *chicken legs and thighs*	(*Evie says not to skimp*
1 *large onion, sliced thin*	*on the pepper*)
1 *lb. can tomatoes*	1 *cup hot water*

Cut the sausages into links, and wash. Prick each link several times with a fork. Fry for 5 minutes in a large covered frying pan (an electric fry pan is excellent for this dish). Use enough water to cover the bottom of the pan. Then remove cover and raise heat until water completely evaporates. If there is not enough fat from the sausages to brown chicken in, add 2 tbs. oil. Add the chicken and onions, and cook chicken until golden, turning parts several times for even cooking. Add tomatoes, parsley, salt and pepper, and hot water. Cook uncovered over medium heat for 30 minutes. Reduce heat to low level, and simmer for an additional 30 minutes.

SERVES 4

Arroz con pollo is a gourmet's blend of tomatoes, chicken, peas, and tasty spices, such as saffron. It is baked in a bed of steaming rice.

❧ ARROZ CON POLLO ❧

1 *broiler-fryer chicken, cut*	1 *medium onion, chopped*
in serving pieces	1 *lb. can tomatoes*
1 *tsp. monosodium gluta-*	1 *lb. can peas*
mate	2 *bouillon cubes*
1½ *tsp. salt, divided*	¼ *tsp. saffron*
½ *tsp. paprika*	1½ *cups uncooked rice*
¼ *cup olive oil*	

Sprinkle chicken with monosodium glutamate, 1 tsp. salt and paprika. Brown in skillet with hot oil. Remove chicken to baking dish with a tight fitting cover. Add onion to skillet, and cook until tender but not brown. Drain liquid from tomatoes and peas; add enough water to make 3 cups. Stir into skillet, scraping brown particles from bottom of pan. Add bouillon cubes, saffron, and remaining salt (½ tsp.). Bring to a boil. Pour over chicken. Sprinkle rice around chicken, stirring so all of rice is moistened. Add tomatoes. Cover tightly. Bake in 350°F. oven for 25 minutes. Uncover, and toss rice. Add peas. Cover and bake for 10 minutes longer.

SERVES 4 TO 6

Chicken cacciatore, or chicken hunter's style, is a favorite Italian dish of which there are many different versions. All versions, however, have one thing in common: they use tomatoes as a base. Many are seasoned with either wine or vinegar. The following three versions include one from Sicily, a popular style cacciatore dish and a rustic one.

◆§ SICILIAN STYLE CHICKEN §◆

1 3-lb. frying chicken, cut in serving-size pieces
1 small onion, sliced lengthwise
3 Tbs. oil
1 small stalk celery, coarsely chopped
1 garlic clove, quartered
1 Tbs. coarsely chopped parsley

1½ Tbs. coarsely chopped fresh basil
⅓ cup dry Marsala
2 Tbs. tomato paste dissolved in ¾ cup warm water
1 tsp. pine nuts
2 tsp. raisins
Salt and pepper

In a large skillet brown the chicken and onion in hot oil until golden. Add celery, garlic, parsley, and basil, and sauté for a few more minutes over moderate heat. Add Marsala, tomato paste in water, pine nuts, raisins, and salt and pepper to taste.

Cook slowly, uncovered, for 40 minutes until sauce thickens. Let this dish rest for 5 to 10 minutes before serving.

SERVES 4

⊷§ CHICKEN ALLA CACCIATORE §⊷

*3½ lbs. frying chicken, cut
  in serving pieces*
2 Tbs. oil
2 garlic cloves
½ cup red wine
*2 cups canned tomatoes
  (1-lb. can)*

*1 large bell pepper, seeded
  and sliced*
*½ lb. fresh mushrooms,
  sliced*
*1 tsp. dried basil leaves, or
  4 large leaves fresh basil*
Salt and pepper

Brown chicken in oil until golden on all sides. Add garlic and allow to brown slightly. Add wine and bring to rapid boil for 2 minutes, turning chicken once. Add tomatoes, peppers, mushrooms, and basil. Bring to boiling point, cover tightly, reduce heat, and simmer gently for 20 minutes. Uncover, and add salt and pepper to taste. Turn the chicken, and cook uncovered for 30 minutes or so to evaporate excess liquids.

SERVES 4

⊷§ CHICKEN ALLA RUSTICA §⊷

*3½ lbs. frying chicken, cut
  in serving pieces*
3 Tbs. oil
*2 large garlic cloves,
  coarsely chopped*
3 Tbs. parsley, chopped

½ cup red wine vinegar
*½ cup canned plum toma-
  toes, or 2 fresh plum tomatoes, chopped*
Salt and pepper

Brown chicken well in a large skillet with hot oil. Add garlic and parsley, and continue cooking over medium heat until garlic turns light yellow. Add wine vinegar, raise heat, and cook until vinegar is nearly evaporated. Add tomatoes, and salt and pepper to taste. Cook, covered, over low heat for 20 minutes. Remove cover, and cook additional 10 minutes.

SERVES 4

Some folks have been known to cook up a chicken just so that they might have a bit left over for this delicious luncheon or second-night tomato treat. Left-over chicken and luscious baking tomatoes are the main ingredients.

⊌§ CHICKEN-STUFFED TOMATOES §∾

4 large, firm tomatoes
1 tsp. salt
1 cup chopped chicken meat
½ cup cracker crumbs
1 egg
1 Tbs. cream

1 tsp. onion juice
Salt and pepper
½ tsp. powdered basil
1 cup chicken stock
4 slices buttered toast

Cut a small slice from the top of each tomato, and scoop out the pulp. Reserve pulp for use in stuffing. Sprinkle tomatoes on the inside with 1 tsp. salt. Remove seeds from reserved pulp, and drain off excess juice. Combine pulp with chicken, cracker crumbs, egg, cream, onion juice, salt and pepper to taste and basil. Mix well, and use to fill cavities in the tomatoes. Arrange tomatoes in a baking dish, and pour stock around them. Bake at 350°F. for 30 to 40 minutes until tomatoes are just tender. While the tomatoes are baking, baste several times with the stock. Serve on slice of hot toast.

SERVES 4

The tomato was brought to the Philippines by Spaniards, and the resourceful natives have added it to one of their most basic and best loved dishes. Cousin Lee Tinniny, who is with the Air Force, sent me this one from the Island Republic.

⊷ LEE'S ADOBO ⊷

1 3-lb. frying chicken
2 lbs. pork
⅓ cup vinegar
Salt and pepper to taste
1 Tbs. soy sauce
1 bay leaf

4 Tbs. oil
4 Tbs. flour (approx.) dis-
    solved in equal amount of
    water
1 can tomato sauce

Cut the chicken and pork into serving pieces. Place in a
large kettle with enough water to cover. Add vinegar, salt and
pepper, soy sauce, and bay leaf. Bring to a boil, reduce heat
and simmer for 1 hour until meat is cooked. Remove meat from
broth and drain well. Measure the broth and set aside. Heat
oil in a large skillet, and fry meat until golden brown. Mix
flour and water (1 tbs. flour for each cup of broth). Add flour
mixture to the broth. Add tomato sauce and simmer until
thickened. Pour over the meat and serve with steamed rice.

SERVES 6 TO 8

An old American favorite is sweetbreads any style, and
Grandma Roth had her own special "tomatoey" way with
sweetbreads in which she used up some of her delicious home-
canned stewed tomatoes.

⊷ SWEETBREADS AND TOMATOES ⊷

2 large sweetbreads
Salt and pepper
Dash cayenne pepper
1½ Tbs. flour
2 Tbs. butter
1½ cup tomatoes, stewed
    (or unseasoned raw)

2 Tbs. green pepper,
    chopped (only if unsea-
    soned tomato is used)
2 Tbs. onion, chopped (only
    if unseasoned tomato is
    used)
1 Tbs. butter

Soak the sweetbreads in ice water until they begin to turn white. Then, in a saucepan, cover sweetbreads with cold water and heat just to boiling point. Remove from the hot water and cool by putting under cold running water. Drain them well, and remove the veins, leaving the top membrane on. Put sweetbreads between two lint-free towels, top with a weight, and leave for several hours.

Put sweetbreads in a saucepan with 2 cups of water. Salt and pepper to taste. Boil gently for one-half hour. In a small pan, mix the flour and butter. Put over a low heat and cook until the mixture browns, stirring constantly. Add this to cooked sweetbreads and their broth, and cook until thickened. Transfer the pan to a 500°F. oven for a few minutes, to brown sweetbreads. Remove sweetbreads to a serving dish. Add to the gravy the stewed tomatoes (if unseasoned tomatoes were used, boil them with the green pepper and onion for 10 minutes, and substitute these). Salt and pepper to taste, and add butter. Bring to a boil and pour over the sweetbreads.

SERVES 4

Ever since the tomato became popular in cookery master chefs the world over have been giving character to the mild flavor of milk-fed veal with just the right touch of tomatoes.

✠ VEAL SCALLOPINE ✦

1½ lbs. veal cutlet, in very
    thin slices (veal scallops)
1 garlic clove
2 Tbs. oil
Salt and pepper to taste

¼ cup canned tomatoes,
    mashed fine
2 green peppers, sliced
½ lb. mushrooms, sliced

Brown the veal and the garlic, which has been finely minced, in a large skillet with oil. Season with salt and pepper. When lightly browned, add the tomatoes, peppers, and mushrooms. Cover and cook over low heat for 20 minutes. Serve veal with sauce poured over it.

SERVES 4

◄§ VEAL ROLLS §►

8 thin Italian-style veal cut-
lets

12 ozs. mozzarella cheese,
cut in thin slices

3 Tbs. grated parmesan
cheese

3 Tbs. finely chopped parsley

Pepper

1 medium onion, chopped
coarsely

3 Tbs. oil

¾ cup dry white wine

3 Tbs. tomato paste (dis-
solved in 1 cup water)

1 lb. can peas, drained

Salt and pepper

On each cutlet put a liberal amount of cheese slices. Sprinkle each with generous teaspoon of grated cheese and parsley. Pepper to taste. Roll each cutlet tightly so that the cheese will not escape. Sauté the onion in a large skillet with the hot oil. When it becomes translucent and soft, add veal rolls and brown on all sides lightly. Add wine and cook over high heat until wine is nearly evaporated. Add the tomato paste in water, peas, and salt and pepper to taste. Cook over low flame for 20 minutes until the veal is cooked through.

SERVES 4

Since time immemorial, or at least since the Chinese boy Bobo burned down the house and discovered that pork was delicious when roasted, the pig has been a symbol of prosperity and joy. To this day many of both Western and Eastern holiday dishes are centered around the pig in some way. The boar's head for Christmas is an old English custom marking the high point of the Yule season, and the Easter ham is eaten as a festive symbol of the spring season. When combined with pork, tomatoes, with their lively red color, have also become a delicious mark of festivities.

✍§ STEWED PORK LOIN ៩

¼ cup finely chopped carrot	2½–3 lb. pork loin
¼ cup finely chopped celery	1 cup dry white wine
1 medium onion, chopped	2 Tbs. tomato paste dis-
coarsely	solved in 2 cups water
1-inch square salt back,	1 large bay leaf
minced very fine	Pepper
3 Tbs. oil	

Sauté in oil the carrot, celery, and onion, to which the salt back has been added, for 5 minutes. Add the pork loin and continue to cook over medium heat until meat is browned on all sides. Add the wine, raise heat, and cook until the wine nearly evaporates. Add the tomato paste dissolved in water and the bay leaf. Pepper to taste. Bring to a boil, cover, reduce heat and simmer gently for 2¼ hours, adding more water if the sauce becomes too thick or if the meat begins to stick. When cooked, remove to serving dish and pour sauce over.

SERVES 6

✍§ PORK ALLA CONTADINA ៩

1 small onion	1 cup canned tomatoes,
1 large sweet green pepper	mashed
3 Tbs. oil	1 tsp. dried basil leaves
8 loin pork chops	Salt and pepper

Chop the onion coarsely. Wash and seed the green pepper.

Slice it into thin strips. Sauté onion and pepper in the hot oil in a skillet large enough to hold the chops. When the onion is soft and becoming translucent, add the chops and sear quickly on both sides. Add tomato, whole basil leaves, and salt and pepper to taste. Stir, blending seasonings into the tomato. Cook over low heat for 35 minutes until chops are done thoroughly. Remove basil leaves. Serve chops with a generous portion of sauce over each.

SERVES 4

Some say that the art of sausage making is as old as the Babylonians. Since that time there have been many different ways of making and cooking sausages, and one of the more pleasant recent innovations is the use of tomatoes, both as a complementary sauce and as a stuffing ingredient.

৺ LOVE APPLE SAUSAGE ৶

1½ lbs. lean lamb or mutton
2 lbs. lamb or mutton fat
3 cups canned, peeled tomatoes
½ cup cooked rice, mashed fine with fork

⅓ lb. cracker meal or matzo meal
2 packages (1 oz. each) poultry or sausage seasoning

Have your butcher grind the lamb and lamb fat twice. To the ground meat add tomatoes, which have been chopped fine. Mix well with the meat. Add rice, cracker, or matzo meal, and seasoning. Mix with hands for several minutes until well blended. Store, covered, in refrigerator for 24 hours before using. When ready to use, shape into patties and fry until golden brown and cooked through. You may easily freeze this sausage in the shape of patties and remove just enough for use when desired.

◄§ STEWED SAUSAGES §►

1 medium onion, minced
    fine
¼ cup chopped carrot
½ cup chopped celery
3 Tbs. oil
2 lbs. thin cheese and pars-
    ley sausage (or Italian
    sweet sausage)

1 cup beef broth
1 Tbs. tomato paste dis-
    solved in beef broth
2 bay leaves
Salt

Sauté with oil the onion, carrot and celery in a medium sized
frying pan. When they are lightly browned, add the sausage,
which may be cut into links if preferred. Prick the sausages
with a fork while they cook. Turn them often. Cook sausage
until browned on all sides. Then add broth, tomato paste, bay
leaves, and salt to taste. Cook over low heat for 1 hour, turning
and stirring occasionally. If stew thickens too much, add a
little water. Before serving, skim off excess fat with spoon.

SERVES 4 TO 6

◄§ TAXCO SAUSAGE CASSEROLE §►

2 1-lb. cans red kidney beans
1 lb. bulk pork sausage
1 cup chopped onion
½ cup chopped green
    pepper

2 garlic cloves, minced fine
Salt
1½ tsp. chili powder
2 cups tomatoes, mashed
2 Tbs. flour blended in ½
    cup water

Drain the beans, reserving ½ cup of the liquid. Fry the sausage in a skillet until some of its oil is rendered out. Add onion,
green pepper, garlic, and salt to taste. Cook for 10 minutes
until the sausage is well browned and the onion is cooked.
Add beans, chili powder, tomatoes, and bean liquid. Cook for

5 minutes over medium heat. Then add flour and water mixture. Simmer gently for an additional 25 minutes. Pour into broiler-proof casserole dish and place under broiler heat for 5 minutes until the top browns and crisps lightly.

SERVES 6

⊷§ GREEK SAUSAGES §⊷

1½ lbs. ground lamb
1 cup moistened bread crumbs
2 garlic cloves, minced fine
½ cup minced onion
½ lb. can tomatoes

1 tsp. cumin seed
3 Tbs. cooking oil
1 lb. can tomatoes
1 small onion, chopped
Salt and pepper

Mix the meat and bread crumbs thoroughly with your hands. Then blend in garlic, onion, tomatoes which have been chopped, and cumin seed. Let this mixture stand in the refrigerator for several hours before cooking. When ready for use, shape into serving-size patties. Fry these in hot oil until golden, turning once. Then add to the meat the 1 lb. can of tomatoes, chopped onion, and salt and pepper to taste. Let this simmer gently for 35 minutes until the tomato forms a thick sauce.

SERVES 6

Beef is one of the more nutritious meats, but most people prefer only the tender parts of the animal. Since the greater part of the cow or bull is not as tender as many of us would like, the tomato, with its inherent tenderizing and taste-provoking qualities, has proved an invaluable culinary aid. Many budget cuts of beef can be used with amazing success by cooking them with tomatoes. Stew meat, for instance, can be toned up to gourmet level by the addition of tomato paste, wine, and mushrooms.

⋅≼ CAULIFLOWER AND STEWED BEEF ≽⋅

1½ lbs. boneless chuck
1-inch square salt back
⅓ cup chopped celery
⅔ cup chopped onion
⅓ cup chopped carrot
2 Tbs. chopped Italian
　parsley
3 Tbs. cooking oil

½ cup red burgundy wine,
　or any hearty red wine
3 Tbs. tomato paste dis-
　solved in 1½ cups water
½ lb. fresh button mush-
　rooms
Salt and pepper
1 package frozen cauli-
　flower

Cut the beef into 2-inch cubes. Mince the salt back very fine. Sauté celery, onion, carrot, parsley, and salt back in hot oil until lightly browned. Add the beef cubes, and brown them on all sides. Add the wine and cook over high heat until it has nearly evaporated. Lower flame, and add tomato paste dissolved in water, mushrooms. Salt and pepper to taste. Stew over a very low flame for 1 hour or until the beef is tender. If the meat begins to stick to the pan, add more water.

Cook cauliflower according to package directions. When tender, drain and transfer to a deep serving platter.

When the beef is tender, spoon it over the cauliflower and top with the sauce. Mix together gently, being careful not to break the cauliflower apart.

SERVES 4

Chopped beef is another inexpensive cut of meat which has been notably enlivened by the tomato. A few seasonings, a touch of tomato and voilà, a company dish.

⋅≼ CALICO STEAK ≽⋅

¾ lb. lean ground beef
¼ lb. ground veal
1 lb. fresh ripe tomatoes,
　seeded, peeled, chopped
Salt and pepper to taste

3 medium tomatoes, sieved
1 small onion, finely minced
1 garlic clove, minced
1 tsp. chopped fresh Italian
　parsley

Mix beef, veal, chopped tomatoes, and salt and pepper to taste. When thoroughly blended, shape into patties of desired size and broil to desired degree of doneness. When the meat is cooked, serve topped with a sauce made by simmering the sieved tomatoes, onion, garlic, and parsley for 10 minutes.

SERVES 4

By adding just the right touch of spice to their beef stew, the Greeks have elevated an ordinary dish to delicate epicurean levels. This dish is particularly enhanced when prepared in the morning and stored in the refrigerator for quick dinner-time serving.

✑ GREEK BEEF STEW ❧

*1½ lbs. stew beef (cubed to
    desired size)*
1 large stalk celery, chopped
1 large onion, chopped
3 garlic cloves, minced
3 Tbs. oil
8 cups water
*1 cup peeled tomatoes,
    broken apart with a fork*

2 large cinnamon sticks
1 tsp. oregano
Salt and pepper
2 large carrots
1 large onion, cut in half
6 small potatoes
*4 Tbs. potato starch blended
    in ½ cup water*

In a large kettle brown the beef cubes, celery, onion, and garlic in the hot oil. When meat is browned on all sides add the water. Bring to a full boil, and skim off any foam from the top. Add tomatoes, cinnamon, oregano, and salt and pepper to taste. Simmer for 1 hour until beef cubes are tender.

Add carrots, which have been cut into strips, onion halves, and whole potatoes. Continue simmering until vegetables are tender when pierced with a fork.

When the vegetables are cooked, add potato starch with water, a little at a time, using only enough of it to thicken stew to desired consistency. Cook for 5 minutes more. Remove to a large serving bowl.

SERVES 6

Sauce does wonders for a nice, lean beef tongue, especially when gently braised with stewed tomatoes and delicate herbs.

✎§ BRAISED TONGUE ξ⁊

1 fresh beef tongue
½ cup diced carrot
¼ cup diced celery
⅓ cup diced onion

1 cup stewed tomatoes
½ tsp. dried marjoram
Salt and pepper to taste
2¼ cups broth from tongue

Put the tongue in a large kettle and cover with cold water. Bring to a boil over high flame. Skim off any foam from top. Reduce the heat and simmer for 2 hours. Remove and cool slightly. Reserve 2¼ cups of the broth from the cooked tongue. Slice the root away from tongue, and remove the skin. Place the tongue in a long baking pan. Top with carrot, celery, onion, tomatoes, marjoram. Salt and pepper, and pour the broth over all ingredients. Cover with a tight lid and bake at 325°F. for 2 hours.

When the tongue is cooked, remove to a large serving platter. Slice for serving. Strain the sauce through a fine sieve. Pour over the sliced tongue.

SERVES 6 TO 8

Steak, pizza-maker's style, is an old Neapolitan favorite. It can also be used with many different cuts of beef, from the most tender to the toughest. One way to get more mileage from that left-over chunk of roast beef is to slice it thick and cook it alla pizzaiola.

~§ STEAK ALLA PIZZAIOLA §~

4 medium steaks, ¾ lb. each   *2 large, ripe tomatoes, sliced*
  and tender   *2 large garlic cloves, minced*
2 Tbs. rendered fat from   *Salt and pepper to taste*
  suet   *1 tsp. oregano*

Sear the steak quickly on both sides in the rendered fat. Add the tomato and the minced garlic. Sprinkle with salt, pepper, and oregano. Fry over low heat for about 10 minutes until tomato cooks down into a thick gravy. Transfer steaks to a serving platter, pour gravy over them and serve immediately.

SERVES 4

The rocky terrain of Greece has lent itself to the raising of sheep rather than of cattle. This pastoral pursuit has naturally occasioned a wide range of tasty lamb and mutton dishes.

~§ EGGPLANT STUFFED LAMB §~

1 small eggplant   *½ tsp. salt*
⅓ cup salt   *2 eggs*
¼ lb. fresh mushrooms   *1 4 to 5 lb. boned leg of*
1 small onion   *lamb*
4 Tbs. olive oil   *Salt and pepper*
1 cup seasoned bread   *2 cups tomato purée*
  crumbs   *1 cup red wine*

Peel the eggplant and cut into 1-inch cubes. Put in a large bowl, sprinkle with about ⅓ cup salt and cover with ice cold water. Let sit for ½ hour, stirring a few times. Drain eggplant and rinse with fresh water. Drain again. Dry the cubes with paper toweling.

Clean the mushrooms with a damp towel. Slice them into small cubes. Sliver onion lengthwise. Heat oil in a medium sized frying pan. Add eggplant, mushrooms, and onion, and fry over medium heat until browned. Remove pan from heat, and add bread crumbs, salt, and eggs. Blend all together well.

Flatten lamb out, with the boned surface facing up. Sprinkle with salt and pepper and spread with the eggplant stuffing. Roll the leg and secure with string. Place in a large baking dish.

Mix the tomato purée with the red wine. When well blended spoon about ⅓ of it over the lamb. Bake in a 350°F. oven until cooked (40 minutes per pound of meat), basting frequently with remaining tomato-wine sauce. When cooked, transfer to a serving platter, remove strings from around meat, and slice. Sauce may be skimmed to remove excess fat and can be served in a gravy boat.

SERVES 4 TO 6

⒮ COUNTRY LAMB ⒢

3 *lbs. lamb shoulder, cut in*
  2-inch squares
1½ *lbs. Feta cheese*
2½ *lbs. fresh tomatoes,*
  sliced thick

2 *Tbs. olive oil*
1 *tsp. marjoram*
1 *tsp. dried mint flakes*
Salt and pepper to taste

Cover the bottom of a buttered baking dish with cubed lamb. Add a layer of cheese and a layer of tomatoes. Sprinkle with oil, marjoram, mint, and salt and pepper to taste. Bake in a 350°F. oven until the lamb is tender.

SERVES 6

≈§ LAMB ATHENIAN §≈

⅓ cup olive oil
3 Tbs. lemon juice
2 tsp. salt
½ tsp. crushed oregano
Pepper
2 lbs. leg or shoulder of
   lamb, cut in 2-inch cubes
½ lb. medium mushrooms
3 medium onions, sliced

4 medium artichokes
4 garlic cloves
Crushed oregano
Boiling water
1 tsp. salt
3 medium tomatoes, quar-
   tered
Avgolemono Sauce*

Marinade: Mix together olive oil, lemon juice, salt, crushed oregano, and dash of pepper.

Pour marinade over lamb, mushrooms and onions in shallow dish. Cover and chill for several hours or overnight, mixing occasionally. Wash artichokes. Place a clove of garlic and dash of oregano in center of each. Place in 1-inch of boiling water in deep saucepan large enough to hold artichokes snugly. Sprinkle each artichoke with ¼ tsp. salt. Cover and boil gently for 35 to 45 minutes or until stems can be easily pierced with fork (add a little more water if needed). Cut off stems. Turn artichokes upside down to drain. Drain lamb and vegetables. Reserve marinade. Skewer lamb and broil 4-inches from source of heat, 5 to 7 minutes per side. Alternate mushrooms, onion, and tomato on skewers. Brush with marinade and broil 3 to 4 minutes per side. Serve lamb and vegetables kebabs with artichokes and avgolemono sauce.

SERVES 4

* AVGOLEMONO SAUCE

3 eggs
¼ cup lemon juice

1 cup chicken stock (or
   bouillon)

Beat eggs in top of double boiler. Gradually blend in lemon juice and warmed stock or bouillon. Cook over boiling water until slightly thickened, stirring constantly. Beat until foamy. Remove from heat and serve hot with artichokes.

MAKES ABOUT 2 CUPS

⋖ ROAST LAMB AND ARTICHOKES ⋗

1 (4-lb.) leg of lamb	2 8-oz. cans Spanish-style
1 Tbs. pure vegetable oil	tomato sauce
1 Tbs. lemon juice	1 cup water
1 garlic clove, crushed	6 small or 3 large artichokes,
2 tsp. oregano	tips and stems cut off, and
1 tsp. salt	chokes removed
½ tsp. pepper	1 lemon, sliced

Rub lamb with a mixture of oil, lemon juice, garlic, oregano, salt, and pepper. Roast in large roasting pan at 400°F. for a half hour. Reduce temperature to 350°F. Baste roast with drippings. Continue roasting 1 hour. Skim off excess fat from drippings. Add tomato sauce and water to roasting pan. Arrange artichoke halves, cut side down, in tomato sauce mixture around the roast. Add lemon slices. Continue roasting 1 hour or until artichokes are tender and lamb is done.

SERVES 4 TO 6

Two ingredients that make Creole cooking unique are tomatoes and rice. This lamb dish makes liberal use of both. It is cooked with tomatoes and served on a bed of rice.

⋖ LAMB SHANKS CREOLE ⋗

4 lamb shanks, about 1-lb.	2 garlic cloves, crushed
each	Salt and pepper to taste
2 Tbs. salad oil	½ tsp. dried marjoram
1 can (1-lb.) tomatoes	¼ tsp. oregano
1 medium onion, sliced	¼ tsp. powdered basil
1 green pepper, sliced	½ tsp. Worcestershire sauce
⅓ cup celery, sliced	4 cups cooked rice

Brown the lamb well in a large skillet, turning so that all surfaces will be cooked. Transfer the meat, drained of its oil, to a large roasting pan. Add the tomatoes, onion, green pepper, celery, garlic, salt and pepper, marjoram, oregano, basil, and Worcestershire sauce. Cover the lamb shanks evenly. Tightly cover the pan and bake at 350°F. for 2 hours. Serve with hot rice.

SERVES 4

❧ LAMB PIE ❧

8 medium potatoes	*Salt and pepper to taste*
1 tsp. salt	*½ cup milk*
2 lbs. boneless lamb	*4 Tbs. butter or margarine*
1 onion, chopped	*1 Tbs. finely minced parsley*
2 Tbs. oil	*Pepper to taste*
½ cup tomato paste diluted	*1 tsp. paprika*
* in 1 cup water*	

Peel the potatoes and boil in salted water (1 tsp. salt) until tender when pierced with a fork.

While the potatoes are cooking, cut the lamb into 1-inch cubes. Brown the meat and onion in the hot oil in a large skillet. Turn often so all sides of the meat are cooked. Drain off the excess oil, and add the tomato paste diluted in water. Salt and pepper to taste. Stew, uncovered, until the meat is cooked and the sauce is thickened.

When potatoes are cooked, drain well and add milk, butter, parsley, and pepper to taste. Mash well, and whip until fluffy. Put one half of potatoes in the bottom of a large casserole dish and smooth into an even layer. Spoon meat and its gravy over the layer of potatoes. Top with rest of potatoes, spread into a smooth layer to cover meat. Sprinkle with paprika. Bake at 350°F. for 30 minutes or until potatoes are well browned on top.

SERVES 4 TO 6

Outdoor barbecueing, though as old as the caveman, has become refined and civilized enough to form an important part of the American cooking scene. Americans have adopted outdoor cookery from many different lands and have added some of their own native flavorings to enhance these unusual dishes.

⊷§ LAMB KEBABS HOISIN ঌ

2 lbs. boneless lamb leg   *1 lb. fresh mushrooms*
Hoisin Bourbon Marinade*

Cut the lamb into 1½-inch cubes. Arrange cubes in a single layer in a shallow dish. Add enough marinade to cover lamb. Chill for 1 hour. Thread lamb cubes and mushrooms on skewers. Broil 3 to 4 inches from source of heat, or cook on outdoor grill for 10 to 15 minutes, turning frequently. (Cooking time depends upon desired degree of doneness.)

SERVES 6

* HOISIN BOURBON MARINADE

1 cup Hoisin Sauce (available in Oriental specialty shops. Cost is about 50¢ for 16 oz.)
1 cup honey
1 cup tomato purée

1 cup Bourbon
1 garlic clove, crushed
1 Tbs. chopped fresh ginger or ½ tsp. powdered ginger
Dash soy sauce

Mix all ingredients together. Cover and chill.

MAKES 4 CUPS

My beautiful wife, Donna, who has a masterful way with food—probably because she is half-French—finds liver an unusually interesting and versatile food. Like many Americans, though, she finds it difficult to eat liver simply fried and not "sauced up." Her favorite liver recipe has a flavorful Creole background which is quite agreeable to her French palate—and those fortunate guests for whom she cooks it.

◆§ DONNA'S FAVORITE LIVER §◆
CREOLE

1½ lbs. beef liver
1 cup flour
¼ cup butter or margarine
1½ cups sliced fresh onions
1½ cups fresh tomatoes,
  peeled and chopped

½ cup diced fresh celery
1 green pepper, thinly sliced
1 tsp. salt
¼ tsp. ground black pepper

Wipe the liver with a damp cloth and cut into thin strips. Coat the strips lightly with flour. Melt the butter or margarine in a large, heavy skillet. Add the liver and sauté until evenly browned. Add the onions, tomatoes, celery, green pepper, salt, and black pepper. Cover and simmer gently for 20 minutes. The sauce may be thickened if desired by adding a small amount of flour and butter roux (blend equal amounts of flour and butter). Stir into the liver mixture and cook until sauce boils and thickens. Serve with the sauce.

SERVES 6

VI

Vegetable Dishes

When Europeans first closely examined the odd vegetation brought from the New World, they tried to fit the curiously different species into plant families already familiar to them.

The tomato proved a stumper. What was it like? How could it be used? European botanists searched all the herbals in existence to find answers to the puzzle. The tomato vine, being a little bit like this plant and somewhat like that, was a particularly hard item to classify. The fruit appeared similar to an apple, but upon closer inspection it didn't feel like one. It truly resembled a berry, but then again it was a fairly large, odd sort of berry. Many a learned botanist scratched his hoary head over the enigma. A sage 16th-century herbalist, a certain Doctor Durante of Rome, directly attacked the problem of the tomato, using all the botanical data available at the time. He examined every aspect of the odd plant and astutely observed, "It is a type of eggplant!"

He went on to describe the fruit of the tomato vine as being "first colored green, but upon ripening becomes in some plants as red as blood and in others the color of gold." The good doctor also called the tomato "frigid," which was tantamount to declaring it inedible. He quickly qualified this statement by noting that the tomato wasn't as frigid as the mandrake, for instance, and could be eaten, "just like the eggplant with pepper, salt and oil." He also cautioned that the love apples "offered little food value and are nutritionally bad."

The good doctor could not have been further from the truth, but we must remember that Europeans in those days knew very little about nutrition. Tomatoes actually contain more vitamins and minerals than most other fruits.

A half cup of tomato juice supplies about one quarter of the daily allowance of Vitamin C recommended by the National Research Council. The tomato is an extremely beneficial part of the daily diet. Very few people realize just how healthful tomatoes are.

A medium raw tomato, which is about 2 inches wide and 2½ inches high and weighs about ⅓ pound, is 94 per cent water and has only 30 calories—a boon for weight watchers. This tomato is two per cent protein, has a trace of fat, contains six carbohydrates, 1,649 International units of Vitamin A, .08 milligrams of Thiamine, .06 milligrams of Niacin, .09 milligrams of Iron and 35 milligrams of Ascorbic Acid (Vitamin C). The United States Department of Agriculture has estimated that, for a well-balanced diet, the average family of four should eat at least 9½ to 10 pounds of citrus fruits, including tomatoes, each week.

Keeping vitamins in tomatoes is a problem that tomato suppliers are constantly aware of. Since the amount of Vitamin C in a tomato is directly related to the amount of sunlight the fruit gets just before harvesting, many growers remove excess foliage that might shade tomatoes and reduce their vitamin content.

A way of making sure that tomatoes remain in top nutritional form was accidentally discovered when suppliers solved another problem, that of shipping the fragile fruit many hundreds of miles to market. The suppliers assumed that, by keeping them at very frigid temperatures, the tomatoes would reach the consumer's table in the best possible condition. However, instead of keeping longer, they ripened prematurely. This unnatural refrigerator ripening caused the fruit to become soft, watery, and easily subject to decay. California tomato growers found that long exposure of green tomatoes to temperatures below 55 degrees caused just such ripening.

Soon growers started to experiment with shipments of tomatoes at higher temperatures. The standards which were subsequently set up resulted in hundreds of thousands of dollars being saved by tomato producers in California, Texas, Florida, and Mexico. These savings have long since been passed on to the American tomato-loving public.

Tomatoes, much like bananas, love a fairly warm environment. But they are a little fussier than bananas. If the temperature is too warm—over 85 degrees, for instance—they will not become a lovely bright red. They should be ripened at room temperature between 60 and 75 degrees. Once ripe, a firm tomato can be stored for about a week at room temperature with very little loss in Vitamin C. As they overripen they tend to lose this vitamin content. The ripe tomato can also be stored for about two days in the refrigerator without deterioration. However, it is still best to buy tomatoes, freshen them up for a few days and then eat them as soon as possible.

When man stumbled upon the art of cooking he discovered a culinary refinement which has its advantages as well as its drawbacks. When cooked, food is rendered more palatable, digestible, and safe. The heat of cooking kills many harmful organisms, such as those which cause trichinosis. But cooking also removes some of the beneficial nutrients in food, especially from vegetables when the water they were cooked in is thrown away. Tomatoes, however, are one of the few vegetables which suffer only a slight loss of valuable nutrients during the cooking process because the water in which tomatoes are cooked is never thrown away.

The nutrients boiled down into tomato sauce are fairly durable. Even if a tomato sauce is served at a later meal, it still carries the minerals it has in solution, despite the fact that constant standing and reheating tends to minimize the amount of food value in most sauces.

The vitamin content in cooked or canned tomatoes and in fresh tomatoes is very similar. One cup of cooked or canned tomatoes contains about 45 calories, 2 grams of protein, 9 carbohydrates, 27 milligrams of Calcium, 1.5 milligrams of Iron, 2,540 International units of Vitamin A, .14 milligrams of Thiamine, .08 milligrams of Riboflavin, 1.7 milligrams of Niacin, and 40 milligrams of Vitamin C.

The advantage of the tomato simmering down to a sauce has proven a tremendous boon to vegetable cookery, both in flavor and food value. Not only does the tomato's beautiful red color and zestful flavor liven up many an otherwise insipid green vegetable, but the nutritional advantages of both vegetables are preserved for the table in a savory sauce.

A very basic tomato sauce, which is also a vegetable dish, is stewed tomatoes. Tomatoes prepared in this fashion can be used to bolster many other dishes or served plain.

⊷§ STEWED TOMATOES §⊶

8 large ripe tomatoes   *Salt and pepper*
3 Tbs. butter or margarine   *¼ cup dry bread crumbs**

Scald the tomatoes in boiling water for 15 to 20 seconds, rinse rinse under cold water and remove the skins. Remove cores, and slice the tomatoes into quarters. Put into an enamel saucepan and season with the butter or margarine, salt and pepper. Stew over a low flame until the tomatoes are soft and have begun to dissolve. Serve in sauce dishes with bread crumbs sprinkled over each serving.

SERVES 4

* If this dish is to be used as a sauce, omit bread crumbs.

Tomatoes themselves need only a small amount of preparation to make a delectable lunch which is as quick and easy as it is economical. The success of this particular dish lies in using the freshest of ingredients.

❧ CREAMED TOMATOES ☙

4 large tomatoes
1 large egg
1 cup seasoned bread crumbs
2 Tbs. butter or margarine
2 Tbs. cooking oil

4 slices fresh bread
4 pats of butter (for toast)
2 Tbs. flour
1½ cups rich milk
2 Tbs. parmesan cheese
Pepper to taste

Peel the tomatoes without scalding. Cut into thick slices. Beat the egg in a shallow bowl. Put the bread crumbs in a second shallow bowl. Dip each tomato slice first into beaten egg, then into bread crumbs. Melt the 2 tablespoons butter and oil in a large skillet. Fry tomato slices quickly, until lightly browned. Turn slices very carefully with a fork so as not to break them. Remove from skillet. Toast the 4 slices of bread. Butter them and place on 4 separate serving dishes. Top evenly with tomato slices. Add flour to skillet and blend with cooking oils until smooth. Add milk, cheese, and pepper to taste. Cook, stirring constantly, over a low heat until sauce thickens. Pour ¼ of the sauce over each toast slice. Serve immediately.

SERVES 4

Color added to an otherwise pale vegetable has been found not only to hearten the eye but the appetite as well. This tasty vitamin-packed hot dish uses the pot liquor in which the green vegetable has been cooked plus tomato purée to create a dish as agreeable to the eye as to the stomach.

⇜ RUDDY CAULIFLOWER ⇝

*1 large head cauliflower**	*1½ cups tomato purée*
3 Tbs. butter or margarine	*½ tsp. powdered basil*
1½ Tbs. flour	*Salt and pepper*

Break the cauliflower into pieces. Soak them in cold, salted water a half hour. Drain, cook in boiling salted water until tender but still firm.

While cauliflower is cooking, melt butter in a small enamel saucepan. Stir in flour until smooth. Add the tomato purée, basil and salt and pepper, and cook over low heat, stirring constantly, until thickened.

When the cauliflower is cooked, drain it well and carefully transfer to a serving dish. Pour tomato sauce over it. Serve hot.

SERVES 6

* You may substitute 2 packages of frozen cauliflower, cooked according to package directions.

⇜ CREOLE CORN ⇝

3 large ripe tomatoes	*1 garlic clove, finely minced*
1 package frozen yellow	*2 Tbs. butter or margarine*
corn	*Salt and pepper*
2 Tbs. finely minced onion	*1 cup raw rice*

Scald the tomatoes in boiling water for 15 to 20 seconds. Cool under cold running water, drain and peel. Remove the cores and chop coarsely. Put tomatoes in a saucepan with the corn, onion, garlic, butter, salt, and pepper. Bring to a boil, reduce heat as low as possible and gently cook, stirring often, until tomatoes form a thick sauce. Cook frozen corn over low heat.

While vegetables are cooking, cook rice in a large quantity of boiling salted water. When tender, after about 20 minutes, drain and rinse well with clear, boiling water. Drain again and arrange in a ring around the outside of a serving dish. Serve the cooked corn in the center of the ring. Bring to the table steaming hot.

SERVES 6

Golden ripe corn and fresh tomatoes not only look good together but they are delicious when cooked with just the right seasonings. It seems probable that the first people to eat these two vegetables in combination were the Aztec Indians of Mexico. As the use of the tomato spread throughout kitchens the world over, more and more varieties of this delicious combination were devised. One recipe calls for a fine aged cheddar cheese from Herkimer County, New York, while another is redolent of savory garlic in true Creole style.

ᴇ§ CORN AND TOMATO CASSEROLE §ᴇ

2 Tbs. butter or margarine
2 Tbs. flour
1¼ cups milk
¼ tsp. French thyme
Salt and pepper
3 ripe tomatoes

1 cup canned corn
⅓ cup shredded Herkimer County cheese or other aged cheddar
¼ cup dried bread crumbs
2 Tbs. butter or margarine

Melt the butter in a small saucepan. Blend in flour until smooth. Add milk, thyme, and salt and pepper. Cook over low heat, stirring constantly, until thickened.

Scald tomatoes in boiling water for 15 to 20 seconds. Cool under cold running water; drain and peel. Remove cores and cut into thick slices.

In a buttered casserole dish, form a layer (about ½ cup) of corn. Top with ½ of the white sauce and ½ of the tomato slices. Repeat layers to use up remaining ingredients, ending with a layer of tomatoes. Top with cheese, then bread crumbs.

Dot evenly with butter and bake at 350°F. for 20–25 minutes until cheese begins to bubble and casserole is cooked through.

SERVES 4

Lima beans, one of the most popular beans in the United States, are native to the New World and were discovered by the Spanish settlers of South America. This delicious bean can make a tasty winter vegetable dish with canned tomatoes.

⋖§ MONTEREY BEANS §⋗

4 slices lean bacon
1 medium onion, coarsely
  chopped

1 cup canned tomatoes (8-
  oz. can), mashed
Salt and pepper to taste
1 package frozen lima beans

Chop the bacon into bite-size pieces. In a medium skillet, cook the bacon until transparent. Add the onion and continue to cook until the bacon and onion are browned. Drain off any excess fat. Add salt and pepper to taste. If bacon is very salty, omit salt. Stir in mashed tomatoes. Cook for 10 minutes. Add the lima beans and continue cooking until beans are tender. Add a little additional tomato juice if necessary to prevent beans from sticking.

SERVES 4 TO 6

My especially dear sister-in-law, Carolyn Lefebvre, of Denver, has a Gallic husband with an inordinate fondness for ratatouille, a delicious blend of tomatoes, garlic, onions, zucchini, eggplant, and fresh peppers. Half-French Carolyn is fond of ratatouille herself, and she prepares it to perfection.

"If you aren't in too much of a hurry," Carolyn advises, "you can steep the squash and eggplants in heavily salted water so that they will lose their bitterness."

◦§ RATATOUILLE §◦

¼ cup olive oil
1 garlic clove, thinly sliced
2 large fresh onions, thinly sliced
2 large fresh green peppers, quartered
1 fresh eggplant, sliced ¼ inch thick
2 garlic cloves, thinly sliced

2 small fresh zucchini, sliced ¼ inch thick
4 large fresh tomatoes, thinly sliced
Salt
Ground black pepper to taste
1 tsp. olive oil

Heat ¼ cup olive oil in Dutch oven. Add one clove garlic. Place vegetables in layers, sprinkling salt and pepper over each layer until casserole is filled. Sprinkle the 1 tsp. olive oil over the vegetables and cook, covered, over low heat for 20 to 25 minutes, gently moving vegetables a few times during cooking. Remove cover and cook for 5 to 10 minutes longer. Serve either hot or cold.

SERVES 8

A Mediterranean-accented fresh tomato and zucchini squash casserole is a very simple one to prepare—if you happen to have an electric skillet handy. If you haven't, you can prepare the dish equally as well by putting the vegetable ingredients into a casserole or covered heat-proof oven ware dish and baking them in a 350°F. oven.

◦§ FRESH TOMATO AND ZUCCHINI §◦ SQUASH CASSEROLE

2 Tbs. olive oil
1 lb. zucchini squash
2 cups thinly sliced fresh onion
1½ tsp. salt
½ tsp. Italian seasoning

⅛ tsp. ground black pepper
5 medium-sized tomatoes
1 tsp. sugar
1 cup shredded Cheddar cheese

Pour oil into an electric skillet. Wash zucchini and slice in ½-inch pieces. Add zucchini to skillet and top with onion slices. Combine salt, Italian seasoning, and black pepper, and sprinkle ½ of the mixture over the onions. Peel tomatoes and slice, crosswise, in ½-inch pieces. Arrange over onions. Sprinkle with remaining salt mixture and sugar. Cover skillet, set temperature at 300°F. and cook for 15 minutes. Remove cover and cook for another 8 minutes or until vegetables are tender and almost all liquid has evaporated. Sprinkle cheese on top, cover and cook for 1 minute or until cheese is melted. Serve immediately.

SERVES 6

Celery has been relished by fastidious diners since Roman times, but until the 16th century the vegetable was considered mostly as a wild herb used for soothing a nervous condition. At that time a growing demand for the plant caused celery to appear on the culinary scene as a cultivated vegetable. Fortunately the tomato was also making its debut, and the two became the basis of a great dish.

⋐§ FRIED CELERY ৪৯

1 bunch celery stalks, preferably from the heart and tenderer parts
1 small onion, thinly sliced
3 Tbs. butter
4 large, fresh tomatoes, peeled, seeded, chopped fine

2 eggs
Salt and pepper
1 cup dry bread crumbs (more if necessary)
4 Tbs. finely minced parsley
2–3 Tbs. grated parmesan cheese
4 Tbs. cooking oil

Wash the celery stalks and remove tough parts and strings. Blanch stalks, which have been cut into 3-inch pieces, in boiling water for 2 to 3 minutes. Drain and cool slightly.

In a large skillet sauté onion in melted butter for 5 minutes until browned lightly. Add the peeled, seeded and chopped tomatoes and stew together for 15 minutes.

Break the eggs into a shallow bowl, salt and pepper to taste and beat until well blended. Put the bread crumbs in a second shallow bowl and blend in parsley. Dip each celery piece into the egg and then into the crumb-parsley mixture. Sprinkle each piece with grated cheese. Fry in hot oil until browned on all sides.

Place the celery on absorbent paper to drain, then transfer to a casserole dish. Pour the tomato sauce over all and bake at 350°F. until thoroughly heated.

SERVES 6

The climate in the balmy southern states bordering the Gulf of Mexico affords lucky inhabitants the opportunity to prepare meals in the open air most of the year. One of the unusual recipes used in outdoor cooking in these states is a delicious kabob made with foods native to the region—fresh tomatoes, shrimp, and avocado.

ᥫ§ GULF TOMATO KABOBS §ᥫ

¾ cup salad oil
¼ cup cider vinegar
½ tsp. minced fresh onions
½ tsp. salt
⅛ tsp. ground black pepper

3 fresh tomatoes, cut in wedges
1 lb. shrimp, cooked and peeled
1 avocado, peeled and cut in wedges

Combine oil, vinegar, onion, salt, and pepper. Blend well. Place shrimp, tomatoes, and avocados in oil-vinegar salad dressing to marinate; chill in refrigerator. Arrange on skewers, alternating tomatoes, shrimp, and avocado. Serve as main dish salad, on lettuce, if desired.

SERVES 6

Neapolitan bean dishes are equally as delicious as Neapolitan tomato preparations, but are less well known and appreciated. When the twain meet the results are gastronomically gratifying for those of us who love delicate flavors. One of the lesser known bean dishes enjoyed by Neapolitans is this simple-to-prepare, economical dish which can be used as an excellent luncheon dish or even in place of a fish course during a formal dinner.

STEWED WHITE BEANS

*2 lbs. fresh canneloni (white
  beans)*
3 large tomatoes
4 Tbs. fresh minced parsley
1 garlic clove, finely minced

½ cup chopped celery
2 Tbs. olive oil
½ tsp. oregano
Salt and pepper
4 large Italian biscuits

Shell the beans and wash well. Put in a large saucepan and add water to cover. Bring to a boil and reduce heat. Simmer gently for 10 minutes.

While beans are simmering, scald the tomatoes in boiling water for 15 to 20 seconds. Cool under cold running water, drain and peel. Remove the cores and seeds. Chop the tomatoes coarsely. Mix with the parsley and garlic and let sit out of refrigerator until ready to use.

When beans have cooked for 10 minutes, add celery. Cook until beans are nearly done. Add tomato-parsley-garlic mixture, oil, oregano, salt, and pepper to taste. Continue cooking until beans are thoroughly cooked. Arrange biscuits in 4 separate serving dishes. Spoon beans over biscuits. Serve hot.

SERVES 4

For many of us the flavor of garden fresh tomatoes delicately baked in a casserole belongs to the past, but the following hundred-year-old American recipe resurrects that long-lost flavor.

·§ ESCALLOPED TOMATOES ᴣ·

6 large, ripe tomatoes   1 Tbs. sugar
1 cup cracker crumbs   ¼ cup warm water
⅓ cup butter or margarine   Salt and pepper

Scald the tomatoes in boiling water for 15 to 20 seconds. Cool under cold running water, drain and peel. Remove the cores and slice thick. Each tomato should yield about 3 slices.

In an oven-proof baking dish put a layer of ⅓ of the cracker crumbs. Dot with ⅓ of the butter. Arrange a layer of tomato slices, using about 6 slices. Sprinkle evenly with 1 tsp. of sugar. Repeat layers until the ingredients are used up. Add water to moisten, and salt and pepper to taste. Cover dish with lid or aluminum foil. Bake for a half hour in a 350°F. oven.

SERVES 4 TO 6

Within the short span of a few minutes a few slices of tomato can become transformed into a dish fit for a king, or a prince at least. All that is needed is a heavy dash of Worcestershire sauce, fine wine vinegar, curry powder, and a hard-cooked egg.

·§ DEVILED BROILED TOMATOES ᴣ·

1 hard-cooked egg, mashed   1 tsp. curry powder
3 Tbs. butter or margarine   ½ tsp. prepared mustard
1 egg, slightly beaten   6 fresh tomatoes
1 Tbs. Worcestershire sauce   Salt and pepper
1 Tbs. wine vinegar   ¼ cup bread crumbs
1 tsp. sugar   Butter or margarine

Combine hard-cooked egg, butter, and remaining ingredients in top of double boiler. Cook over hot water for 3 to 4 minutes, stirring constantly until mixture thickens. Remove from heat and allow to stand while broiling tomatoes. Cut tomatoes in half. Sprinkle lightly with salt, pepper, and bread crumbs and dot each with butter. Arrange in broiling pan. Broil tomato halves on lowest rack in broiler until crumbs brown. Arrange on heated platter and top each with deviled sauce.

SERVES 6

Whenever you come across the word "Florentine" in a recipe you know immediately that spinach is among the ingredients. This quick and unusual vegetable dish is uncomplicated, and yet it can make a festive addition to any meal.

✎§ BAKED TOMATOES FLORENTINE §✎

6 fresh tomatoes
1 lb. fresh spinach
⅓ cup soft bread crumbs
1½ tsp. salt
¼ tsp. ground black pepper

6 strips crisp bacon,
crumbled
¾ cup soft bread crumbs
1½ Tbs. bacon fat

Wash tomatoes and scoop out the centers. Turn upside-down to drain. Wash spinach and place in saucepan without water. Cover and cook for 3 to 5 minutes or until leaves are wilted and tender. Drain, if necessary, and chop fine. Add bread crumbs (⅓ cup), salt, ground black pepper, and bacon. Spoon into drained tomatoes. Combine ¾ cup bread crumbs with bacon fat and sprinkle over tomatoes. Bake in preheated oven at 350°F. for 20 minutes or until crumbs are brown. Serve at once.

SERVES 6

Stuffed tomatoes can make a memorable vegetable side dish to balance a meal. Tomatoes can be stuffed with a number of foods; however three of the most often used are bread crumbs, rice, and cheese. The following recipes are a bit complicated, but their flavor will prove worth the additional effort. In the first you will find the secret of success is in parboiling the rice. This helps to remove excess starch.

◄§ RICE-STUFFED TOMATOES §►

8 firm tomatoes	*Salt and pepper*
1 cup raw rice	*8 small slices gruyère cheese*
½ cup chicken broth	*2 tsp. fresh parsley, very*
Pinch of saffron	*finely minced*
1 Tbs. oil	*2 tsp. French thyme*

Slice off the tops of the tomatoes, and scoop out the seeds and pulp. Reserve both tops and pulp for later use. Turn the tomatoes upside-down while preparing the filling.

Strain the pulp of the tomato and discard the seeds.

In a large quantity of boiling water, parboil the rice for 5 minutes. Drain well and rinse under warm water. Return the parboiled rice to the saucepan, and add the broth, pulp and juice of the tomatoes, saffron, and oil. Salt and pepper to taste. Bring to a boil and simmer for 15 minutes until the rice is tender.

While the rice mixture is cooking, prepare the tomatoes by placing in each a slice of cheese and a sprinkle of parsley and French thyme. When the rice is cooked, fill the cavity of each tomato with the mixture. Cover each tomato with its top. Arrange in a buttered baking dish and bake, covered, at 350°F. for 25 minutes. Remove cover and continue baking for 10 minutes more. Serve hot.

SERVES 4

⚜ TOMATOES STUFFED ⚜
WITH MUSHROOMS

4 large, firm tomatoes
¾ lb. fresh cultivated mushrooms
3 Tbs. soft bread crumbs
2 Tbs. beef broth
3 sprigs Italian parsley

1 garlic clove
3 Tbs. cooking oil
1 large egg
2 Tbs. grated parmesan
   cheese
Salt and pepper

Peel the tomatoes without scalding, and cut them in half. Scoop out the seeds and pulp, and reserve for later use.

Clean the mushrooms with a damp towel and slice into hammer shapes. Add the broth to the bread crumbs, and let mixture sit until all the moisture is absorbed.

Mince the parsley and garlic very fine, and mix together.

Heat oil in a large skillet. Add mushrooms, parsley and garlic, and sauté for 5 minutes. Strain tomato seeds and pulp, and discard seeds. Add this strained pulp to mushrooms and cook for 2 to 3 minutes longer. Remove pan from flame and add bread crumb-broth mixture, grated cheese, and egg. Salt and pepper to taste. Stuff tomato halves with this mixture and arrange in a shallow, buttered baking dish. Bake at 350°F. for 35 to 40 minutes until the tomatoes are tender.

SERVES 4

The Neapolitan husband of my sister, Ann Della Cava, has a virtually uncontrollable passion for Eggplant Alla Parmigiana. This delectable dish is not quite the sort of oil-soaked viand served up in short-order Italian restaurants. They prepare their version the easy way, usually with the skin left on the eggplant. Yet, for a superb meatless vegetable dish, there is absolutely nothing that can surpass this casserole, swimming in its own ambrosial liquid. It takes some time to prepare, but the resultant savory platter can be eaten hot or ice-box cold—and there are some, such as myself, who prefer it this way, especially when the weather is warm and sultry.

◄§ EGGPLANT ALLA PARMIGIANA §►

1 large eggplant
2 Tbs. olive oil (a good,
  light oil should be used)
1 small garlic clove
½ can (4-oz.) tomato paste
1 lb. can tomatoes
1 Tbs. sugar
2 eggs

Salt and pepper
1½ cups dry bread crumbs
  (more may be needed)
¼ cup all-purpose flour
4 Tbs. cooking oil
Parmesan cheese
Mozzarella cheese
  (optional)

Peel the eggplant and cut into ¼-inch slices. Arrange in layers in a large bowl. Sprinkle each layer generously with salt. Cover with ice water and place a dish on top to keep all the eggplant slices submerged. Let sit at room temperature for 1 hour to remove the bitter eggplant juices.

While the eggplant is soaking, prepare the sauce. Heat olive oil in a saucepan. Brown garlic lightly, then add tomato paste, and fry for 2 minutes. Add 1 cup of warm water, tomatoes, and sugar. Simmer gently, uncovered, for 1 hour or longer if desired. Remove garlic clove. Strain sauce through a medium sieve.

When eggplant is ready, drain salted water from slices, rinse each slice thoroughly and pat dry with paper towels. Break the eggs into a shallow bowl, add the salt and pepper to taste and beat lightly until well mixed. In a similar bowl, put bread crumbs and flour. Mix the two well. Dip the eggplant slices first into egg mixture, then into bread crumbs. Coat well on both sides. Fry, several slices at a time, in the hot oil. When browned on both sides, drain on absorbent paper.

Spoon 3 to 4 tablespoons of the tomato sauce into a lightly oiled casserole. Arrange a layer of breaded eggplant slices in a dish. Top with generous ladle of sauce and sprinkling of grated parmesan cheese. Repeat this procedure until all eggplant slices are used. End with a layer of sauce. Sprinkle with parmesan cheese and top with mozzarella if desired. Bake in a 350°F. oven for 30 minutes until sauce begins to bubble and cheese melts. Remove from oven and let sit for at least 10 minutes before serving.

SERVES 6 TO 8

Note: If you choose to use mozzarella cheese on top of your casserole you should use only a fresh, wet mozzarella from a cheese store. These cheeses are unsalted and will lend a delicate flavor to your dish. If you use a processed cheese, such as might be found in a supermarket, it will tend to be rubbery and too salty for the delicate eggplant.

Tomatoes and eggplants harmonize so beautifully that they form almost lyrical dishes together. This should not seem strange because the eggplant and the tomato are botanical cousins. Yet the eggplant, like the tomato before it, is slow in coming into favor among English-speaking people. The reason for this aversion is not difficult to understand. Eggplant when merely stewed or boiled is reduced to an almost insipid mass of vegetable matter. Even its grayish brown color repels many people. Eggplant when fried is another matter, and often is heartily accepted when offered to guests.

The following arrangement of fried tomato and eggplant, both separate yet forming a delicious vegetable course, is a particular favorite with many who do not like eggplant in any other way.

CRISP EGGPLANT AND TOMATO

1 small eggplant	¾ cup flour
4 small tomatoes, ripe but firm	1½ tsp. salt
	1 tsp. oregano
4 tsp. sugar	3–4 Tbs. oil

Peel the eggplant and cut into ½-inch slices. Arrange in layers in a deep bowl. Sprinkle each layer with a liberal amount of salt. Cover with ice water and place a dish on the top to keep the eggplant submerged. Allow to stand for 45 minutes to 1 hour.

Cut the tomatoes into ½-inch slices. Sprinkle each slice with the sugar. Mix the flour, salt, and oregano.

When the eggplant is ready, drain well and dry each slice thoroughly. Dip the eggplant and tomato slices into the flour mixture, coating evenly.

Heat the oil in a large heavy skillet. Fry the eggplant over moderate heat until lightly browned on both sides, about 2 minutes on each side. Remove to a platter and place in a warm oven to keep hot. Then fry the tomatoes for about 1 minute on each side. Add more oil if needed.

Top each eggplant slice with a slice of fried tomato.

SERVES 6

An inspiration for the weary eater who has dined on ordinary fare for so long that he has become bored with food is the tangy taste of tomatoes and bell peppers swimming in savory seasonings. The dish is so self-sustaining that it can be a lunch in itself, served over bread rusks. Or it may be the vegetable livener of an otherwise ordinary dinner.

⋘ PEPPERS AND TOMATOES ⋙

2 soft, ripe tomatoes
5 bell peppers
1 small onion, thinly sliced

3 Tbs. olive oil
1 tsp. dry basil
Salt and pepper

Peel and seed the tomatoes. Chop into small pieces. Clean, seed, and slice the peppers. Sauté the peppers and onions in the hot oil until the onions are translucent. Add tomatoes and seasonings. Cover and let simmer over very low heat for 10 to 15 minutes, until the tomatoes form a sauce. Remove from the flame, uncover, and set aside for 5 minutes. Serve with soft Italian bread or rusks.

SERVES 4

VII

Pasta, Egg, and Grain Dishes

"The triumph of the tomato has given hungry men and women a new lease of pleasure. Sad and drear were the days when the gourmet thought to feast, and the beautiful scarlet fruit had no place upon his table. . . . What, indeed was life, what the gift of eating before the Columbus of the kitchen had discovered the tomato, the turkey, and the yellow Indian corn? Reflect upon it, and be grateful that you, at least, were not born in the dark age of cookery!"

These lavish words of praise were written by Mrs. Elizabeth Pennell, wife of Joseph Pennell, the famous American etcher. Mrs. Pennell was a 19th-century epicure who had a keen appreciation of the many roles love apples played in the kitchens of the world.

Today, so vast is the range of dishes in which tomatoes are featured that it is difficult even to classify recipes in one category or another. Many tomato dishes are sufficient unto themselves, such as pizza and pasta.

Pasta, which characterizes southern Italian cooking, is primarily a food of desperation contrived by resourceful chefs who made the most from a bit of flour, water, a minimum of meat, and seasonings. The tomato, because of the very mutability of its flavor, was a prime ingredient in pasta dishes. All a poor man has to do to change the entire tone of a tomato-pasta dish is add a little of the costlier foods such as meat, sausage, or fish. The basic flavoring of a tomato sauce often comes from an extremely tough cut of meat which could be stewed and made tender in a tomato sauce that simmers for hours, such as a typical Neapolitan *'rraú*, a Neapolitan dialect word for sauce. This tomato sauce could then be used with a flour and water pasta that has been molded into any one of over a hundred odd shapes, each shape catching the flavorful tomato sauce in a unique way, thereby creating a different taste sensation—or at least the illusion of one.

Pasta without tomato, to paraphrase an old maxim, is like a very cloudy day—bearable, yet soulless. Pasta is a magnificently simple preparation of flour and water. The best pasta is made from finely ground semolina flour (the very best sort is grown in the American Midwest). Semolina is the refined middlings of hard durum wheat and is rich in gluten, the main protein component of cereals. If you do not have semolina, good pasta can be made from all-purpose flour or, better yet, from bread flour.

Preparing homemade pasta, which puts to shame all store-bought varieties, is a very simple task which peasant women in Italy perform nearly every day. The basic pasta recipe calls for 4½ cups of flour, three eggs, three tablespoons of olive oil, and an ample amount of warm water. The flour, semolina or otherwise, is put on a rolling board, and a well or depression is formed in the center of it. The eggs and oil are dropped into the well, and the flour is worked into them a little at a time. The dough is then moistened with enough water to form a stiff dough. When making pasta, you should knead the dough until it is smooth and elastic, and then cover and allow it to rest for one hour. If semolina flour is used, lengthen the resting time to two hours. The pasta can then be rolled out and shaped into whatever forms are desired. Once the preliminary pasta is made, a tomato sauce can be used to create culinary magic.

Tantalizing tomatoes, masterfully cooked with eggs, have caused more than one *Esquire trenchant,* officiating at formal banquets, to be the subject of mouth-watering oohs and ahhs as he presented such delicate fare before appreciative dinner guests. For some rarer alchemic and culinary reason the egg reaches heights of excellence when combined with tomatoes. Such delicate dishes as eggs creole and eggs piperade, which are much appreciated by gourmets, were first the fancies of simple folk who loved two good foods—tomatoes and eggs— and decided to combine them.

What we call sawdust pudding or just plain corn meal mush is also the base for a savory Mediterranean dish popular in northern Italy, Corsica, and to some extent, in France. This tasty pudding, called "polenta," differs from corn meal mush in that it is often cooked with grated parmesan cheese or other flavorings and is served cold, in oblong or diamond-shaped strips. It is often covered with a thick, delicious tomato sauce. Many other sauces and foods are also used with polenta. Napoleon I, like a true Corsican, loved his polenta, particularly when served with tender little roasted thrushes or warblers in a delicate white wine sauce, each little bird perched atop his own tiny polenta nest.

Polenta is much older than Indian corn, which arrived in Europe about the same time as the tomato and was instantly snatched up and eaten by Europeans, particularly in polenta dishes. Before the arrival of corn, polenta was made with chestnut flour, which is smoother to the tongue than corn meal. In parts of northern Italy and in Corsica some polenta dishes are still made with this delicious flour.

The most popular modern American tomato and cereal dish, rivaling the great pastas, is pizza. Pizza American-style is so well known that it needs no explanation. American pizza originated in anthracite coal-burning ovens which produced a steady, even heat that baked bread to perfection. Unfortunately for us, today's pizza is prepared in gas-burning metal ovens which for some unknown reason cannot bake bread in the way that heat in coal-burning ovens can.

Pizza came to America with the early southern Italian immigrants who made their own bread and brought it to a bake shop to be baked slowly and perfectly with anthracite coal. Mamma would often bring her children with her, and to keep them quiet she brought along her own pizza makings—sauce, left-over sausage or salami, and cheese. The pizza would be cooked quickly, and it kept the children fairly quiet while the bread baked.

As times changed and immigrants became more affluent they stopped making their own bread and bought it from the baker. Some bake shops also sold pizza containing ingredients which were plentiful in the United States—tomatoes, mozzarella or scamozza cheese, and oregano. The pies were still baked in the brick ovens, and the results were superb. Soon, some bakers stopped making bread and concentrated on making American-style pizza.

In Naples, where legend says that pizza was first popularized, there were reports of pizza as early as the 16th century when Basile, the Boccaccio of Naples, mentioned a dainty called a "pizzelle" in one of the *novelle* he wrote in the rich Neapolitan dialect. These dainty delicacies, however, were prepared from a sweet cake-like dough and covered with a marmalade.

The time of the true origin of pizza is far earlier than the 16th century, and pizza is a dish which cannot be claimed solely by the Neapolitans. The very word "pizza" is derived from the Latin term *picea,* which means "pitch" or "tar" and was used to describe a type of rustic pasty which the Romans ate. The *picea* was probably filled with a pitch-like or gooey substance such as cheese. During the flow of time the word was transformed in northern Italy to *pinza* which meant a "pasty" and in southern Italy to *pizza* which was also used to describe a rustic cake. The word "pizza" today, even in Italy, is not used exclusively for an unsweet, tomato pie. There are many, many different types of pizza, with tomato and without, and both sweet and unsweet.

The history of the American pizza, however, still has a Neapolitan background because the Neapolitans were the first to discover and make use of the plum tomato. Around the 18th century the pizza again flared into popularity, and the first mention was made of a Neapolitan pizza which used tomatoes. The French Revolution was raging about this time, and the old order was tumbling down. In Neapolitan kitchens a parallel but less violent revolution was raging because of the discovery of the unique tomato. Italians writers at this time thought so much of the new event that mention was made of the remarkable fact that Neapolitans were using an "extremely tasty, pear-like" tomato.

The discovery of the plum tomato revolutionized tomato cookery because it is a variety that lends itself to cooking far better than most other types of tomatoes. The plum does not break down as easily as most tomatoes, and when it is used in salads its skin is tender enough to be eaten. Because of these qualities the Neapolitans began using plum tomatoes almost exclusively in their cooking.

The Bourbon kings of Naples were formidable eaters in the grand Neapolitan manner, and they dearly loved their spicy tomato dishes, especially pizza. Moreover, like good Bourbons they tended to copy their regal kinsmen on the throne of France. They imitated French courtly manners, and since Marie Antoinette was noted for performing housewifely tasks such as milking the cows and baking (in the grand manner of course), the Neapolitan queen, Maria Carolina, also performed housewifely tasks in an equally grand manner. She dutifully prepared pizza for her family and favorite courtiers.

For reasons of their uniqueness, the hard-to-classify recipes in this chapter are more difficult to prepare than most tomato dishes. This is either because of their cooking procedure or because of the type of ingredients used in their preparation. Certain cereals such as rice and flour would appear to be easily interchangeable. All-purpose flour might do very well for a basic pizza dough, yet, for really proper results, hard flour or bread flour must be used. For ordinary pasta the flour should be semolina. Yet, again, all-purpose flour may be used with satisfactory results. Rice, a seemingly ordinary grain, actually isn't ordinary. True, one can use American long grain rice in a risotto, but the dish is not nearly as exquisite as when Italian rice is used. "Good cooks can make even stones taste delicious," an old Sicilian proverb says, but despite the greatest culinary skill a dish will suffer if the proper ingredients are not used. If you substitute similar ingredients, the product may be adequate and possibly quite good. Yet, the soul of the platter, the essence of the recipe, will somehow suffer.

One of the most interesting of all pizza is the Sicilian pie which uses a concentrated tomato purée called *strattu* (or "extract") in Sicilian. This *strattu* is not quite as thick as tomato paste and forms the basis of a delicious sauce made with anchovies and oregano.

Sicilian pizza is a rare treat which is seldom made in the United States. Most pizza sold as Sicilian pizza here is a rustic type of thick crust pie commonly made all over southern Italy and called *pizza alla casalinga* or "homemaker's pie." It resembles the American pizza in that the chief ingredients are scamozza or mozzarella cheese, peeled plum tomatoes or sauce, oregano, and grated cheese. The only similarity between the homemaker's pizza and Sicilian pizza is the thick, deliciously doughy crust.

There are two types of basic Sicilian pizza, both extremely popular in Palermo, the ancient royal capital of Sicily. One is an ancient pizza which uses a sweet-sour tomatoless sauce, and the other is a fragrant tomato pie.

❧ SICILIAN PIZZA ❧

1 package active dry yeast	4 to 5 cups bread flour
1½ cups warm water	6 Tbs. tomato paste
2 tsp. salt	½ cup plus 2 Tbs. water
1 Tbs. oil	1 can anchovy fillets with oil

1 *garlic clove*   ¼ *tsp. ground black pepper*
2 *tsp. dry oregano*   1 *Tbs. olive oil*

In a large mixing bowl dissolve yeast in warm water. Let stand for a few minutes then add the salt and the oil. Mix well. With an electric mixer, gradually blend in 2½ cups of the flour. When well mixed, scrape beaters to remove all dough. Blend in remaining flour, stirring with a wooden spoon until a thick dough is formed. Turn dough out onto a floured board and knead until smooth and elastic. Place dough in a bowl which has been lightly oiled and brush top lightly with oil. Cover with a towel and let rise in a warm place for approximately 2 hours or until dough has doubled in bulk.

While dough is rising, prepare the sauce. In a small saucepan, blend tomato paste and water. Stir in anchovies and their oil. Mince garlic very fine and add to tomato mixture along with oregano and black pepper. Cook over a medium heat until the anchovies have completely dissolved, for about 5 minutes. Set aside to cool.

When the dough has risen, turn out onto a lightly floured board and knead several times. Have ready a lightly oiled pan, about 12 inches by 16 inches with 2 inch sides. Place dough in pan and spread out evenly with oiled hands so that the dough covers bottom of pan. Cover dough with sauce, spreading evenly to within ½ inch of the edges. Brush the edges with olive oil. Set in a warm place to rise for about 30 minutes. Bake in a preheated oven at 350°F. for 35 to 45 minutes until the bottom crust has browned evenly. Remove from the oven and serve piping hot.

SERVES 4 TO 6

The oldest Neapolitan pizza, considered by many to be the only true tomato tart of Naples, is an extremely simple dish which tastes quite different from our American version. No cheese is used. The sauce is a delicious variation of Marinara sauce made of peeled plum tomatoes, garlic, olive oil, and oregano, which are spread over top of dough before baking.

⟨§ NEAPOLITAN PIZZA §⟩

1 package active dry yeast
1½ cups warm water
2 tsp. salt
1 Tbs. oil
4 to 5 cups bread flour
1 large can tomatoes (about
  2 lbs.), preferably peeled
  plums

6 garlic cloves
2 tsp. oregano
2 Tbs. light olive oil
Kosher salt (large grain)
Freshly ground black pepper

Prepare the dough as for Sicilian Pizza. When dough has risen, turn out onto a floured board and knead several times. Have ready 2 12-inch round pizza pans, lightly oiled. Divide the prepared dough into 2 equal parts. Spread each portion evenly over the pans. The edges should be slightly thicker than the rest of the dough.

While the pizza dough is rising, prepare the remaining ingredients. Drain the tomatoes, and slice each one into 4 fillets. Set aside in a covered bowl. Mince the garlic as fine as possible.

When the dough is ready and prepared for baking, arrange the tomato fillets evenly over each pie. Sprinkle ½ of the garlic over each pie and sprinkle with the oregano, olive oil, Kosher salt and pepper to taste. Bake in a 375°F. oven for 20 minutes until the bottom crust has browned evenly.

SERVES 4 TO 6

Pizza is as magnificent a platter in the summer as it is during winter, and the Neapolitans make sure that they take full advantage of the season in their pizza baking. They prepare a pizza similar to our American variety except that all the ingredients, including the spices, are fresh. They are particularly fussy about the type of cheese used on their pizza and prefer mozzarella so fresh that it is dripping wet with whey. In the United States it is impossible to get a mozzarella that fresh except in Italian sections where they prepare their cheese daily. Supermarket mozzarella is very dry and is in reality very like scamozza. Scamozza cheese is good for pizza, but for magnificent results use fresh, wet mozzarella.

⌁ SUMMER PIZZA ϡ

1 package active dry yeast	1 large wet mozzarella
1½ cups warm water	cheese
2 tsp. salt	3½ Tbs. olive oil
1 Tbs. oil	4 large sprigs fresh oregano
4 to 5 cups bread flour	Kosher salt (large grain)
1 lb. fresh plum tomatoes	Freshly ground black pepper

Prepare the dough as for Sicilian Pizza. When dough has risen, turn out onto a floured board and knead several times. Have ready 2 12-inch round pizza pans lightly oiled. Divide the prepared dough into 2 equal parts. Spread each portion evenly over the pans. The edges should be just a little thicker than the rest of the dough.

While the pizza dough is rising, prepare the remaining ingredients. Scald the tomatoes in boiling water for 15 seconds. Cool under running water and peel. Cut into small pieces. Drain the cheese and slice into thin pieces.

When the dough is ready and prepared for baking, arrange the tomato pieces evenly over the pies. Top with cheese slices. Sprinkle olive oil over each. Wash oregano sprigs well and mince very fine. Sprinkle over pies. Then sprinkle them with salt and pepper to taste. Bake in a preheated oven at 375°F. for 20 minutes until the bottom crust is well browned.

SERVES 4 TO 6

When Italy was united there were no jolly Neapolitan queens to make pizza, and the delicacy suffered a slight decline until a June visit made to Naples in 1889 by the King of unified Italy, Umberto I and his Queen, Margaret. Both the king and queen were well acquainted with northern Italian and French cooking but were very curious about Neapolitan fare. The queen, in particular, was especially interested in pizza and wanted to taste it. Arrangements were made with the most famous local pizza baker in Naples to honor the queen with his art. History has ascribed the honor of baking Queen Margaret's pizza to two men, Raffaele Esposito and Peppino Brandi. You can take your pick as to which was the actual hero of the day, but legend has it that the queen was given three different types of pizza to taste. She was delighted.

"They were all excellent," she said, "but I prefer the one made with mozzarella, tomato, and basil."

There is more than a hint, however, that mere gustatory joy was not the good queen's only reason for picking the cheese, tomato, and basil pizza. The dish also reflected patriotic motives because the white of the cheese, the red of the tomatoes, and the green of the basil were the colors of unified Italy's national flag.

⊷§ QUEEN MARGARET'S PIZZA §⊶

1 *package active dry yeast*	1 *large wet mozzarella*
1½ *cups warm water*	*cheese*
2 *tsp. salt*	*Kosher salt (large grain)*
1 *Tbs. oil*	*Freshly ground black pepper*
4 *to* 5 *cups bread flour*	8 *large leaves basil, or 4 tsp.*
1 *large can (approx.* 2 *lbs.)*	*powdered basil*
peeled plum tomatoes	

Prepare the dough as for Sicilian Pizza. When dough has risen, turn out onto a floured board and knead several times. Have ready 2 12-inch round pizza pans, lightly oiled. Divide the prepared dough into 2 equal parts. Spread each portion evenly over the pans. The edges should be just a little thicker than the rest of the dough.

While the dough is rising, prepare the remaining ingredients. Drain the tomatoes. Pass whole tomatoes through a coarse sieve to remove all seeds. Set aside in a covered bowl but do not refrigerate. Drain the cheese and cut into thin slices. If using fresh basil, wash the leaves thoroughly and mince very fine.

When dough is ready and prepared for baking, spread each pie evenly with strained tomato pulp. Top with slices of cheese. Sprinkle evenly over pies salt and pepper to taste, and the basil. Bake in a preheated oven at 375°F. for 20 minutes until the bottom crust is browned evenly.

SERVES 4 TO 6

The rich cuisines of France and Italy merge in the border provinces of both nations, and many of their dishes are similar both in sound and taste, particularly those of the Riviera. In Nice and adjacent towns they cook a French pizza which reflects a common culinary heritage. This dish, called "pissaladiere," is a delightful square pizza which makes use of luscious anchovies packed in oil, onions, toothsome black olives, and tomatoes.

◦§ PISSALADIERE §∾

½ package active dry yeast
¾ cup warm water
1 tsp. salt
1½ tsp. oil
2 to 2½ cups bread flour
1 lb. can tomatoes, preferably plum
1 tsp. butter or oil

1 Tbs. chopped onion
1 tsp. basil
1 tsp. oregano
1 garlic clove, minced very fine
1 can anchovey fillets packed in oil
¾ cup pitted black olives

Prepare the dough as for the Sicilian Pizza, but use one-half of the amount indicated for each ingredient. When the dough has doubled in bulk, turn it out onto a lightly floured board. Punch down. Stretch the dough to fit a lightly oiled 8 by 12 inch pan.

Break the tomatoes into small pieces with a fork or potato masher. Add the butter or oil, onion, basil, oregano, and garlic. Simmer over low heat for 10 minutes. Let this mixture cool to lukewarm before using.

When cooled, spread tomato mixture over dough evenly. Arrange anchovy fillets over the top, then brush edges of dough with oil from anchovies. Cut black olives into halves and arrange over pizza also. Bake in a preheated oven at 400°F. for 20 minutes until the bottom crust is evenly browned.

SERVES 4

Eggs, the ancient symbol of life's renewal, become magnificent gourmet dishes when cooked with tomatoes. Rich in protein, eggs are often used as a meat substitute, especially for lunch. Many an otherwise uninspired midday meal is raised to an almost regal repast when a simple egg dish made with tomatoes is used.

⋘§ EGG AND TOMATO CUPS §⋙

¾ cup minced onion	*Salt and pepper*
3 Tbs. butter or oil	*8 large eggs*
8 tomatoes	

In a large skillet, sauté the onion in the hot butter or oil until onion is transparent but not browned.

While onion is cooking, scald the tomatoes in boiling water for 15 seconds. Cool under cold running water and peel. Cut cores from tomatoes and remove any defective parts. Sieve the tomatoes through a coarse strainer or food mill. Add the sieved tomato mixture to the onions. Salt and pepper to taste. Simmer over low heat for 5 minutes.

Break 8 eggs into tomato mixture and mix with a fork until eggs are cooked to desired degree. When cooked, spoon into 4 custard dishes.

SERVES 4

In Westhampton Grandma Julia Davis Roth made this delicious scrambled egg and tomato dish for her large family on many an autumn afternoon. It is a recipe which helped her use up some excess cream from the cow, eggs from the chickens, and fresh, crimson tomatoes from the garden.

❧ EGGS ROTH ☙

10 eggs
½ cup fresh cream
Salt

Freshly ground black pepper
1 lb. fresh tomatoes, peeled
* and quartered*
3 Tbs. butter or margarine

Break the eggs into a bowl. Add the cream, and salt and pepper to taste. Beat with a fork until the whites and yolks are just blended. Heat the tomatoes in a small saucepan until hot but not cooked. In a large skillet heat the butter or margarine until melted. Pour in the egg mixture and gently stir until they are set. When eggs are cooked, stir in the hot tomatoes. Serve immediately.

SERVES 6

The French have more egg recipes in their culinary repertoire than any other people in the world. They fry, bake, roast, simmer, boil, stew, and steam eggs, but one of the tastiest ways a Frenchman cooks his eggs is in an omelet, a truly superb culinary invention. When the tomato was introduced into French cuisine, an unusual dish capable of being eaten at any time of the day came into being.

✑§ TOMATO OMELET §✑

1 cup stewed tomatoes	*8 large eggs*
½ tsp. sugar	*Salt and pepper*
½ tsp. fresh chopped basil	*3 Tbs. butter or margarine*

Drain the stewed tomatoes and use only the pulp. Add the sugar and fresh basil. Put in a small saucepan and bring to a boil.

Break the eggs into a bowl, and add salt and pepper to taste. Beat the eggs with a fork until the whites and yolks are just blended. Melt the butter in a heavy skillet. When very hot, pour eggs into pan and reduce heat to medium. Cook until top of omelet is nearly set, then spread hot tomato mixture over ½ of the eggs. Fold in half so that the tomato is sandwiched between two layers of egg. Transfer to a heated platter.

SERVES 4

The day after Easter is usually a time when the average household larder is richer by a dozen or so hard-cooked brightly colored eggs. If you ever wonder how you can get away from making the inevitable egg salad, try serving them as a hot dish that will serve not only as a family lunch but as a hot supper as well. All that is needed are tomatoes, spices, and a Bell pepper.

✑§ HOT DEVILED EGGS §✑

1 small green Bell pepper	*1 tsp. Worcestershire sauce*
1 small onion	*2 drops Tabasco sauce*
3 Tbs. butter or margarine	*⅔ cup milk*
1 Tbs. flour	*6 hard-cooked eggs*
1⅓ cups canned tomatoes,	*¼ cup soft bread crumbs*
chopped	*2 Tbs. butter*
1 tsp. salt	

Wash the Bell pepper and mince fine. Mince the onion. Heat the butter or margarine in a heavy skillet, and sauté the vegetables until lightly browned. Stir in the flour and mix until evenly blended. Add the tomatoes, Worcestershire, Tabasco, and salt. Stir until blended. Simmer over low heat until tomatoes thicken.

Stir the tomatoes into the cold milk. Slice the eggs. Add very carefully to the tomato-milk mixture. Turn into a greased baking dish.

In a small frying pan fry bread crumbs in butter. When they are light brown and crisp, sprinkle them over tomato-egg mixture. Bake at 375°F. until browned on top, about 15 minutes.

SERVES 4

Eggs are extremely adaptable to the various nuances of different national cuisines. The following egg dish was originated by the Basques, who live on the border between France and Spain. They have adapted the magnificent Spanish sofrito and used it as the basis for fluffy, soft and extremely good scrambled eggs. Sofrito means cooking certain foods, such as onions, peppers, and garlic over a low heat so that they are simmered down to almost a purée. This purée is used as the savory base and thickening for many Spanish dinners.

⊷§ EGGS PIPERADE §⊶

1 large onion
3 Tbs. butter or oil
6 Italian green peppers,
  seeded and chopped
1 garlic clove, finely minced
  or crushed

1 lb. fresh ripe tomatoes
Salt and pepper
6 eggs
1 Tbs. fresh chopped parsley

Chop the onion and in a heavy or cast-iron skillet slowly cook in butter or oil until the onion begins to soften but not brown.

Add the green peppers and garlic, and continue cooking until the vegetables are very soft. Do not allow to brown; stir often to permit even cooking. Scald the tomatoes in boiling water for 15 seconds. Cool under cold running water and peel. Remove cores and chop fine. Add the tomato to the onion-pepper mixture. Salt and pepper to taste. Continue cooking, covered, until the tomatoes are dissolved and a purée is formed.

Break the eggs into a bowl and beat with a fork until the whites and yolks are thoroughly blended. When the tomato purée is ready, pour the eggs into it and mix gently with a fork until the eggs are nearly set. Spoon immediately into a serving dish. These eggs should not be allowed to harden. Garnish with the chopped parsley.

SERVES 4 TO 6

Long grain rice has been a New Orleans favorite for a good many years, accompanying so many Creole dishes that many people feel the two go together. Tomatoes and peppers are other favorite Creole ingredients. When these three are combined with eggs, you have a very special dish which can make a great supper on some cold winter's evening.

~§ EGGS CREOLE ?~

3 Tbs. chopped onion
3 Tbs. chopped green pepper
2 Tbs. melted fat or oil
1½ cups cooked or canned
*   tomatoes*

⅔ cup water
⅓ cup uncooked rice
½ tsp. salt
Pepper
4 eggs

Cook the onion and green pepper in fat in a large frying pan until the onion is lightly browned. Add the tomatoes and water, and heat to boiling.

Add the uncooked rice, salt, and pepper. Cover and cook over low heat until rice is tender, for 25 to 30 minutes. Stir occasionally with a fork to prevent sticking. If the rice becomes dry, add a little more water.

Drop eggs on rice and cover. Simmer for 5 to 10 minutes or until eggs are as firm as desired.

SERVES 4

Polenta, like pasta, is a food of poor people with ingenious minds who discovered how to create a great meal from the bare essentials. All one needs for a decent polenta is corn meal, salted water, and some tomato sauce. Polenta can be, and often is, a dish which uses up the left-over tomato sauce so universally used throughout Italy, though more so in the south than in the north.

POLENTA WITH TOMATO SAUCE

¼ cup diced salt pork
1 large garlic clove
2 Tbs. olive oil
½ can tomato paste
1 can tomatoes (1 lb.)
Salt and pepper

½ tsp. dry oregano
2 leaves fresh or dry basil
1 cup corn meal
1 quart boiling water
1 tsp. salt

Parboil the salt pork in 2 cups water for 5 minutes. Drain. Slice the garlic clove in half and sauté with the salt pork in hot oil. When the garlic is light brown, add the tomato paste and fry for additional 2 minutes, stirring constantly. Add the tomatoes, salt, pepper, oregano, and basil. Simmer gently for about 1 hour. Remove the garlic, and strain the sauce. Pour the strained sauce into a saucepan and continue simmering until the corn meal is done, for about ½ hour. Add more water if needed.

Stir the corn meal into the 1 quart of boiling water. Add the salt and cook until thick, for about 30 minutes. Spoon the polenta into 4 soup dishes. Top with the sauce.

SERVES 4

Polenta is primarily a northern Italian staple where it is served with any number of different sauces and meats. But it is also a popular dish throughout Italy. Sausages are also used throughout Italy and have been made on the Peninsula since Roman times. One of the most popular polenta dishes combines sausages, polenta, and grated cheese.

✑ POLENTA WITH SAUSAGES ⋗

1 small onion	*½ tsp. dry oregano*
2 Tbs. oil	*Salt and pepper to taste*
1 lb. sweet Italian sausages,	*1 cup corn meal*
(about 8 links)	*1 qt. water*
1 6-oz. can tomato paste	*1 tsp. salt*
3½ cups warm water	*3 Tbs. grated locatelli cheese*

Mince the onion fine. Heat the oil in a deep saucepan or skillet, and brown the onion and sausages. Add the tomato paste and fry for 2 minutes. Add the warm water, oregano and salt and pepper to taste. Stir until well blended and simmer gently for 1 hour. Add more water if the sauce thickens too much.

Thirty minutes before the sauce is done, stir the corn meal into the boiling water. Add salt and cook until thick, for about 30 minutes. Pour into a loaf pan. Top with the sausages and a generous amount of the sauce. Sprinkle with the cheese. Bake in a preheated moderate oven (350°F.) for 15–20 minutes.

SERVES 4

Risotto is a one-pot dish that closely resembles the paella of Spain. Risotto, however, contains delicious Italian rice. Italian rice is unique, and many people in the United States have never eaten it. It is a comparatively rare rice even in Italy, being a short grained variety not quite as shiny or bright as the pearly white Carolina rice grown and eaten here. But without Italian rice a good risotto suffers. If the Italian rice cannot be obtained and American rice is substituted in the following two recipes, the liquid should be decreased slightly.

◄§ RUSTIC RISOTTO §►

4 or 5 sprigs fresh parsley
1 sprig fresh rosemary
1 sprig fresh marjoram
1 small onion
¼ lb. chunk Genoa salami
2 Tbs. oil
3 Tbs. tomato paste

¼ cup chopped carrots
½ cup chopped celery
1⅔ cups Italian rice
5⅛ cups water, very hot
Salt and pepper
3 Tbs. grated parmesan
* cheese*

Wash parsley, rosemary, and marjoram, and mince fine. Chop the onion and salami. Heat oil in a heavy skillet, and sauté the parsley, rosemary, marjoram, onion, and salami until all are lightly browned. Add the tomato paste and stir until blended. Add the carrots and celery, and cook for a few more minutes. Add the rice, and fry, stirring constantly for 2 minutes. Add the hot broth, salt and pepper to taste and bring to a boil. Cover, reduce heat to low and cook for 15 minutes until the rice is tender. When cooked sprinkle with the grated cheese and serve immediately.

SERVES 4

Mushrooms, especially when fresh, are welcome additions to any meal, but in a risotto made with tomatoes they are as nearly divine as a food can get. This risotto is an economical, easy-to-prepare dish which is a favorite in the port city of Genoa. It is often a substitute for polenta or pasta.

❧ GENOAN RISOTTO ❧

1¾ cups rice
7 cups boiling water
3 Tbs. oil
1 small onion, chopped
½ lb. fresh mushrooms
1 cup peeled tomatoes

½ tsp. dry basil
Freshly ground black pepper
Salt
3 Tbs. grated parmesan
  cheese

Stir the rice into the boiling water and parboil for 5 minutes. Drain reserving the water. In a heavy or cast-iron skillet, sauté the onion in the oil until translucent. Clean the mushrooms with a damp cloth and slice into hammer shapes. Add to the onions and sauté until browned. Mash the peeled tomatoes with a fork and add to the mushrooms and onions. Cook for a few minutes, then add the rice. Simmer for 5 minutes, then add the water in which the rice was parboiled. Bring to a boil, add the basil, salt, and pepper to taste. Cover, reduce heat to low and simmer until the rice is cooked. Sprinkle with the grated cheese and serve immediately.

SERVES 4

The frugal Tuscans are as artful with their food as they are with palettes and sculptor's chisels. In Tuscany any bit of food can be turned into a substantial supper, especially if one uses one's own best judgment. A few eggs, some stale bread, an onion, a cucumber, and a few tomatoes can make a delicious supper. There are some chefs who compare this dish with a gazpacho that has not been pounded in a mortar and blended. In any case it is extremely tasty, and I like it as well as does any Tuscan.

☙ TUSCAN BREAD SLICES ❧

2 large eggs
8 slices stale Italian bread
1 large sweet onion
Vinegar, preferably cider
1 lb. fresh ripe tomatoes

1 large cucumber
2 leaves fresh basil
3 Tbs. light olive oil
Salt and pepper

Hard cook the eggs and cool under cold running water. Put the bread slices in a deep pan in one layer only. Add enough water to cover and let stand for 10 minutes. Slice the onion and put in a bowl. Add enough vinegar to cover. Peel the tomatoes without scalding and slice into thick wedges. Peel the cucumber and cut into round, ¼-inch slices.

When the bread is ready, gently squeeze out the excess water and break into tiny bits with a fork. Put the bread into a serving bowl. Add the onions along with a little of the vinegar in which they were soaked. Chop the basil leaves. Add the tomato wedges, cucumbers, basil leaves, oil, salt, and pepper. Peel and slice the eggs. Add to the bread mixture. Toss gently and serve immediately.

SERVES 4

Spaghetti is probably the most widely-known Italian staple in the United States and is most frequently served with a tomato and meatball sauce. Yet spaghetti and meatballs are rarely eaten in Italy. The long thin strands of pasta are used with many other unusual sauces. One of the lesser known spaghetti dishes takes full advantage of the lush juiciness of summer tomatoes and fresh herbs. Freshness is so highly prized in this recipe that the tomatoes are not even cooked.

⌁ SPAGHETTI WITH FRESH ⌁ TOMATOES

5 large firm tomatoes
4 sprigs fresh parsley
2 large leaves basil
1 garlic clove

1 Tbs. oil
1 lb. thin spaghetti
Salt and pepper
3 Tbs. light olive oil

Put on a large kettle of salted water to boil for the pasta. Scald the tomatoes for 15 seconds in a small kettle of boiling water. Cool under cold running water and peel. Cut the cores out, remove the seeds and cut into eighths. In a mortar, pound the parsley, basil, garlic and 1 tbs. oil to a fine paste. When the water is boiling, add the spaghetti to cook according to directions on package. When done, drain and transfer to a large serving dish. Add the tomato fillets, the parsley-basil-garlic paste, and olive oil. Salt and pepper to taste. Toss gently and let stand for a few minutes.

SERVES 4 TO 6

Lightly cooked tomatoes often make sauces which are superb with pasta. These sauces catch the essence of fresh tomatoes without long, violent cooking, and summer sweetness is retained in the flavor of the dish. In the region of Puglia in Italy they favor a very special meatless sauce made with fresh herbs, tomatoes, garlic, and sweet Italian peppers, all gently cooked and served over thumb-size pasta.

⌁ PASTA WITH FRESH PEPPERS ⌁

10 Italian sweet peppers
4 Tbs. olive oil
1 lb. fresh plum tomatoes
1 garlic clove
¼ cup chopped fresh parsley

12-oz. box ziti macaroni
Salt and pepper
2–3 Tbs. grated romano cheese

Wash the peppers, and remove the seeds. Slice into quarters.

Heat the oil in a large heavy skillet, and sauté the peppers until they have softened slightly. Remove with a slotted spoon and set aside in a bowl. Scald the tomatoes in boiling water for 15 seconds. Cool under cold running water and peel. Remove the cores and chop coarsely. Mince the garlic and parsley. Add the tomatoes, garlic, and parsley to the skillet in which the peppers were cooked. Simmer over a medium heat for 15 minutes.

Cook the ziti according to the directions on the package. When nearly cooked, add the peppers to the tomato mixture in the skillet. Continue cooking. When the ziti is cooked, drain well and place in a large serving dish. Pour the sauce over the ziti and toss. Salt and pepper to taste and sprinkle with the grated cheese. Mix again and serve.

SERVES 4 TO 6

The forty-day fast of Lent was a very austere season during the early days of Christianity. People fasted rigorously and were forbidden to eat the flesh of warm- or cold-blooded animals, including fish and water fowl. Even butter and eggs were considered of animal origin and were not eaten. When the tomato came upon the table during those gastronomically severe days it was a welcome respite from the hard Lenten fast.

Just before the Lenten season arrived it became customary to use up all the forbidden foods in the house. Many celebrations grew up around this bit of kitchen cleaning. Shrove Tuesday in England, Mardi Gras in France, and Carnevale in Italy were all the same day on which feasting and merriment reigned and everyone had his last taste of meats and fats. In Naples a special dish was devised in order to use up these foods, and it was so delicious that as the Lenten rules gradually relaxed the dish continued to be made. This special Carnevale dish is a lasagne casserole far different from any you would normally order in an Italian-American restaurant. It is a very simple creation, yet it seems complicated, since it requires a great deal of time to prepare all the formerly banned Lenten foods which go into it.

⊷ CARNEVALE LASAGNE ⊱

2 Tbs. chopped salt pork
¼ lb. sweet Italian sausage
  (about 2 large links)
1 garlic clove
1 can tomato paste
2 cans warm water
1 (1 lb. 12-oz.) can peeled
  plum tomatoes
1 tsp. dry oregano
4 leaves fresh or dry basil
Salt and pepper
4 eggs
½ lb. ground beef
1 slice stale bread
Milk
1 small egg, slightly beaten
1½ Tbs. grated parmesan
  cheese

½ clove finely minced garlic
¼ cup cooking oil
5 slices Genoa salami
1 lb. lasagne noodles
2 Tbs. cooking oil
2 lbs. fresh ricotta cheese
3 eggs, slightly beaten
3 sprigs fresh parsley
4 Tbs. grated parmesan
  cheese
1 small unsalted, wet
  mozzarella cheese
1 large unsalted, wet
  mozzarella cheese
¼ cup grated parmesan
  cheese

First, a tomato sauce should be prepared. Parboil the salt pork in 2 cups water for 5 minutes. Drain. In a large, deep kettle over a low flame render the pork until most of its fat has liquefied. Pierce the sausage links several times with a fork and add to the kettle. Raise the heat to medium, and brown the sausage on all sides. Add the garlic clove and cook until light brown. Add the tomato paste and fry for 2 minutes, stirring several times. Add the warm water, peeled tomatoes, oregano and basil. Salt and pepper to taste. Cover tightly and simmer gently for 1½ hours, stirring two or three times to prevent sticking. Remove the sausages from the sauce and set aside. Discard the garlic clove. Pass the sauce through a coarse sieve or food mill and return to the kettle. Simmer uncovered for about 30 minutes until the sauce has thickened slightly.

While the sauce is simmering, prepare the remaining ingredients. Place the eggs in a small saucepan, and cover them with cold water. Put eggs on to boil over high flame. When they reach the boiling point, remove from the flame and cover. Let eggs sit for 15 to 20 minutes. Drain the hot water from them and cover with cold water. Allow to cool.

Put the ground beef in a mixing bowl. In a separate small dish, place the slice of bread. Cover with milk and let sit until thoroughly moistened. Drain and mash into small pieces. Add to the meat along with the egg, 1½ tbs. grated cheese, ½ clove minced garlic. Pepper to taste. Shape into small balls, about 1-inch in diameter, and fry in a heavy skillet in ¼ cup oil, turning so as to brown on all sides. Remove from the pan with a slotted spoon and set aside.

Cut the salami into small pieces, about 8 per slice. Slice the sausage links into small rounds.

Put the lasagne noodles into a large kettle of boiling salted water to which 2 tbs. oil has been added. Add one at a time to avoid their sticking together. Cooking time will vary with the type and thickness of the noodles, but they should be allowed to cook until nearly, but not quite, *al dente* "to the tooth," or firm to the bite. The remainder of the cooking will take place in the oven.

While the pasta cooks, mix the ricotta cheese with the beaten egg until thoroughly blended. Wash parsley and mince fine. Add to the ricotta cheese along with parmesan cheese. Slice small mozzarella into small pieces, about 1½-inches long and ¼-inch wide. Add to the ricotta and sprinkle in pepper to taste. Mix until well blended.

Peel hard-cooked eggs and carefully cut into thin slices. Try to keep the slices whole. An egg slicer is recommended.

Drain the large mozzarella cheese and cut into thin slices.

When the lasagne noodles are ready, drain and rinse each one with cool water. Place in a colander to drain for a few minutes.

To prepare the lasagne you will need a large (about 12 by 16 inches) rectangular pan with deep sides. A cake pan would suit the purpose well. Lightly oil the bottom and sides of the pan. Ladle in a generous portion of the tomato sauce enough to cover the bottom. Arrange a layer of noodles over the sauce. Top noodles with a layer of the ricotta cheese mixture, then another layer of noodles. Next, top with a layer of meatballs, salami, sausage, and eggs. Add a layer of noodles, then another generous ladle or two of tomato sauce to cover the noodles. Repeat these layers until all ingredients are used, ending with a layer of noodles and a layer of sauce. Top with the slices of mozzarella cheese, then sprinkle with the ¼ cup grated cheese. Bake in a preheated oven at 350°F. for 35 to 45 minutes until the cheese is browned and the noodles are tender when pierced with a fork. Remove from the oven and let sit for 10 minutes before serving.

SERVES 6 TO 8

Spaghetti with meatballs, which to many Americans is typical Italian food, is like American pizza; very few Italians eat it. Meatballs often accompany other Italian pasta dishes but are rarely served mixed with string-like spaghetti. Coils of pasta served with large orbs of chopped meat is an esthetically displeasing grouping of foods to Italian chefs. They prefer to blend properly formed pasta artistically with properly formed meatballs, which are often tiny.

◈§ PASTA WITH MEATBALLS §◈

1 onion
2 Tbs. oil
2 cups peeled, seeded and chopped tomatoes
3 leaves fresh basil
1 lb. ground lean beef
2 Tbs. finely minced parsley
2 Tbs. grated parmesan cheese
1 egg, slightly beaten

Salt and pepper to taste
½ cup finely broken, soft bread crumbs, moistened with 2 Tbs. milk
1 clove garlic, finely minced
3 Tbs. oil
1 lb. maccaroncelli or ziti macaroni
¼ cup grated parmesan cheese

Slice the onion into thin lengthwise strips. Heat the oil in a medium size saucepan and fry the onion until lightly browned. Add the tomatoes and basil leaves. Simmer covered for 20–30 minutes while preparing the meatballs.

Combine in a bowl meat, parsley, 2 tablespoons grated Parmesan cheese, egg, salt, pepper, bread crumbs, and garlic. Mix well with a fork. Shape into tiny (1-inch diameter) meatballs. Heat the 3 Tbs. oil in a heavy skillet and fry the meatballs slowly until firm and brown on all sides. Remove from pan with a slotted spoon and add to the tomato sauce. Simmer gently until the pasta is ready, about 15 minutes.

Boil the pasta according to the package directions. Drain well and place in a large serving bowl. Cover with sauce and meatballs. Top with the ¼ cup cheese. Toss gently and serve at once.

SERVES 4 TO 6

VIII

Fancies

Grandma Julia Davis Roth had a unique way of describing the many unclassifiable relishes, pickles, sauces, preserves, candied fruit, and other specialty items which flowed from her farm kitchen during harvest time. Grandma liked plain talk that spared her a great deal of lengthy explanations, and when it came to putting up preserves plain talk described that activity best. It also removed unnecessary vanity, she thought, from what to her was a simple and pleasurable farm chore. Grandma was a farm woman who developed her cooking skills through long years of standing over a coal stove. On this old coal stove were prepared delicious foods, many of which were winter preserves that people in this sophisticated age might find only in gourmet food shops.

"Fancies" was what Grandma Roth called the tasty treats she made in her sunny Westhampton kitchen. "Fancies" was

Grandma's way of describing the unique food items which she annually put up for winter with a minimum of words. "Fancies" was Grandma's way of describing the unique food items which she annually put up for winter with a minimum of words. "Fancies" was a good word to Grandma, and since it describes best the dishes in this chapter, "fancies" they shall be.

Grandma Roth made fancies for the same reason that farmers' wives who lived for hundreds of years before her did. It was a way of preserving food from a plentiful harvest for the lean winter months ahead. Grandma was creative in her kitchen, as was her mother before her. She had many tried-and-true recipes handed down to her, carefully written in a well-worn "receipt" book.

Tomatoes came high on her list of cooking chores for late autumn because Grandpa Roth loved tomatoes and grew the finest, juiciest love apples in Westhampton. The only trouble with putting them up was that tomatoes had the annoying faculty for ripening almost all at once and kept ripening until the first frost arrived. This natural phenomenon kept Grandma Roth and the six little Roths busy canning and putting up all sorts of tomato fancies. When the first frost did come, Grandpa would pull up the tomato vines, roots and all, and tie them to the rafters of the entry way, next to the kitchen. There the green tomatoes would ripen in the dark and blush crimson red among the wilted green leaves of the tomato vine. Grandma would wait until some of the "entry way tomatoes" ripened and she would then turn them into chili sauces, relishes, and other delicious fancies.

Grandpa Roth was not the first man to be partial to the lusciousness of a good ripe tomato or tomato fancies, nor was he the last man. The love of the tomato is a passion shared by the inhabitants of the four corners of the globe. The famous French gourmet, Brillat-Savarin, noted that "the pleasures of the table belong to all ages, to all conditions, to all countries and to every day."

The same philosophy applies to the assorted dainties which are created from the universal tomato. The kitchens of many nations have contributed to tomato cookery and have enriched tables the world over. Nowhere has the impact of this rich heritage been more keenly felt than in the United States, where cooks have added and adapted to the American palate literally hundreds of tomato recipes. Not only was this adaptation inspired by the viand-wise city epicure but by the American farmer's wife as well, who eagerly used these foreign tomato recipes. One of the most important steps in preparing tomato fancies came from Europe, and credit must be given to the man who made it possible for Grandma Roth to keep Grandpa Roth happy.

It was a Frenchman, Nicholas Appert, discoverer of the art of canning in 1795, who deserves thanks for his great service to mankind and particularly to tomato lovers. Monsieur Appert was a brilliant man possessed of many unique virtues that enabled him to become the father of the modern tin can and the champion of the contemporary dinner table. Just imagine how long it would take to prepare a modern meal without canned food. Meals can be made in the fraction of the time they once took because this genial gastronome, chef, and inventor discovered a method of preserving food in cans and glass jars.

Appert was a resourceful chef who had an absolute passion for tomatoes in any form, but unfortunately he could only have them in season. The inventor, besides being a professional cook, was a confectionery maker and a chemist. His fondness for love apples made him persevere in his experiments at his Paris confectionery shop until he discovered a way to enable man to eat tomatoes all year round. For his invaluable discovery he received a prize in 1809 from a grateful French government. Appert's principle of canning tomatoes came from the same scientific concept which was later popularized by Dr. Louis Pasteur—that fermentation and decomposition of organic substances could not take place if air were excluded (from a jar of tomatoes, for example) by creating a vacuum with heat.

Peter Durand, developer of the first tin can, transported Appert's invention to the British Isles in 1810. American fish processors adopted the marvelous invention in 1819, and canned salmon and lobsters were soon being sold. In 1823 an American, Thomas Kensett, invented a tin can that could be used to pack all types of food, and by 1847, tomatoes were being commercially canned for domestic consumption in Jamesburg, New Jersey.

Today, most tomato fancies are an "accompaniment" food which can be eaten with hot meals or used to garnish cold platters. They are also bright reminders of summer. This latter characteristic was particularly appreciated by the Roth family. Fancies livened up winter meals and were so highly regarded that when autumn rolled around, everyone gladly helped to make them. The activity was fun and not quite as difficult as it may seem. Tomato fancies are easy to prepare even though many people today mistakenly believe that putting up jars of preserves and relishes is a hard, old-fashioned job.

Some people even fear that preserving tomatoes is dangerous. Nothing could be further from the truth. Love apples have a built-in natural safeguard—their high acid content— that helps to preserve them. Two common substances used in pickling and preserving tomatoes—vinegar and sugar—also help to deter bacterial growth and add pleasant flavor.

Cleanliness, of course, is another important factor in successful home-canning. The jars used for storage should be washed, rinsed well and then boiled, to sterilize them. This does not mean that expensive equipment must be used. For instance, junior-size baby food jars which have been cleaned and boiled for 10 minutes are excellent for packing chili sauce. The hot chili sauce will create a vacuum in the jars as it cools, and you will hear a tiny pop as the tops seal. This pop indicates that the seal is complete. These baby food jars have small rubber gaskets around their lids which allow this successful canning. They will keep the chili for months as fresh and sweet as the day it was made. These jars, however, cannot be used for all types of canning; they should be used only when the recipe calls for large quantities of vinegar or sugar.

Many of the best tomato preserves are made with the smaller varieties of love apple. The plum, currant, cherry, pear, and red and yellow peach tomatoes are much sweeter than the larger size love apples, and are closer to being berries than vegetables. For this reason they are much sought after for making different types of fancies. The tiniest of these small tomatoes is the cherry-size, sweet-sour strawberry tomato. This yellow berry grows encased in a husk that resembles a miniature Japanese lantern and is often called "ground cherry" or "husk tomato." This tasty bitter-sweet berry is also highly prized by confectioners and is sold in specialty stores and vegetable markets. Gardeners find it the easiest of all tomatoes to grow because it is a self-seeder and produces new plants season after season.

One of the more foolhardy bits of devilment that Grandpa Roth's children dared was to steal husk tomatoes from his favorite pie patch. Strawberry or husk tomatoes meant one thing to Grandpa—some of Grandma's delicious pie, warm from her oven and cooling on the table. Heaven help those who hindered his having that pie on the table!

Strawberry Tomato Pie is an unusual dessert treat that is rarely made now because of the scarcity of husk tomatoes in the supermarkets. If you are lucky enough to be near a specialty store or ambitious enough to raise some of these fruits in your own garden, you can experience an unusual delicacy. This little tomato is the sweetest of the tribe and tastes more like a wild berry than a tomato. Caution is advised in cooking this tomato pie. The berry's skin is very tender. Grandpa liked them whole and preferred that the delicate little love apples remain that way in the pie. Excessive heat will burst their skins, and they should be carefully watched so that they can retain their shape and full juiciness.

◄§ STRAWBERRY TOMATO PIE §►

1 cup sugar
⅔ cup water
¼ cup cornstarch blended in
   2 tbs. water
1 tsp. fresh lemon juice

6 cups strawberry tomatoes,
   washed and left whole
1 baked pie shell with decorative pieces for ornament*

In a saucepan, mix the sugar and water. Place over medium heat and bring to a boil. Allow to boil rapidly for several minutes, then stir in the blend of cornstarch and water. Return to a boil, stirring constantly. Reduce heat and cook until mixture is thick and clear. Stir in the lemon juice and tomatoes. Return to a boil, then remove from the heat immediately. Let cool slightly, then pour into the pie shell. Decorate with the pieces of baked pie crust. Allow to cool for 1 hour, then refrigerate until well chilled.

SERVES 6

* PIE CRUST

1½ cups all-purpose flour
½ cup cold margarine
¼ tsp. salt
1 Tbs. brandy

1 to 2 Tbs. ice water
1 Tbs. melted butter
   (optional)

With a pastry blender or two knives, cut the margarine into the flour. When well mixed and of a mealy consistency, add the salt and mix well. Then moisten with the brandy and ice water, mixing with a fork until the dough will form a ball. Chill the dough for 1 hour. Roll out the chilled dough, reserving about ⅓ of it for decorations, on a floured pastry board. Fit into a 9-inch pie plate. Flute the edges, and prick evenly around the inside with a fork.

Roll out the remaining third of the dough on a floured board and cut into decorative shapes to ornament top of pie. Transfer with a spatula to an ungreased pan for baking.

Bake the crust at 400°F. for 15 minutes or until it is evenly browned. Remove from oven and cool thoroughly before using. You may brush the baked shell with the melted butter while it is still hot, if you like. This will impart a buttery taste and a richer texture to the shell.

MAKES 1 CRUST PLUS ORNAMENTS

Pies make the meal for any good French-Canadian and are often eaten for breakfast, lunch, and supper. They are served both in dessert form and as part of the main repast in such dishes as tourtière, a tasty spiced, minced pork pie. Mince pie, though English in origin, was adopted by the French-Canadians as one of their favorite desserts. As much as they loved mincemeat, the French-Canadians are religious people and staunch Roman Catholics, and since mincemeat contains flesh, the good Canadians did not eat the pie on Fridays according to the former Church rule of abstinence from meat on Fridays. But mince meat was so beloved that they created a special Friday pie made of green tomatoes that closely resembles the original.

✑§ MOCK MINCEMEAT PIE ﾟ

4 cups green tomatoes,	*¼ tsp. allspice*
washed and chopped	*¼ tsp. coriander*
¾ cup seedless raisins	*¼ tsp. salt*
1⅓ cup brown sugar	*2 cups all-purpose flour*
2 Tbs. cider vinegar	*⅔ cup cold shortening*
½ tsp. ground cloves	*½ tsp. salt*
½ tsp. ground nutmeg	*5 or 6 Tbs. ice water*
1 tsp. cinnamon	*2 Tbs. melted butter*

Put the tomatoes in a large kettle and set over a low heat to cook for several hours until they are soft. Stir often to prevent sticking. When done, add the raisins, brown sugar, vinegar, cloves, nutmeg, cinnamon, allspice, coriander, and salt. Simmer an additional 40 minutes.

During the last 10 minutes that the mincemeat is simmering, prepare the pie shell. Cut the shortening into the flour until well blended using either a pastry blender or two knives. Add the salt and mix well. Add the ice water a little at a time and mix well until the dough forms a soft ball. Divide the dough into 2 parts, one a little larger than the other. Roll out the largest part on a floured pastry board until it is very thin. Arrange in a 9 inch pie plate. When the mincemeat is cooked, stir well and pour into the pie shell.

Roll out the second part of dough as thin as the first. Place over the filling, press the edges together to seal. Cut steam vent in top crust; trim edges. Bake in a preheated oven at 425°F. for 10 minutes, then reduce heat to 375°F. and continue baking for another 20 minutes.

SERVES 6

The first candy civilized man tasted was fruit, simmered slowly in honey until it was translucent and crystallized. This candied fruit would keep for a long time and was highly thought of by the ancient Greeks and Romans. One of the little-known attributes of the love apple is its ability to be made into a superb candied fruit.

⊷§ CANDIED PLUM TOMATOES §⊷

1 *lb. ripe plum tomatoes*	*Pinch powdered cloves*
1 *cup brown sugar*	*Confectioner's sugar*

Scald the tomatoes in boiling water for 15 seconds. Cool under cold running water and slip skins off. Remove the cores. In a large saucepan, slowly melt the brown sugar. Add the cloves, tomatoes and gently coat with the melted sugar. Cook, covered, over a very low heat until tomatoes are candied and clear. Transfer to a cookie sheet. Set in a low oven at 200°F.

to dry. The drying time is determined by the tomatoes. Check every 30 minutes. They should have the texture of dried dates when done. Remove from the oven and coat each lightly with the confectioner's sugar. Pack between layers of waxed paper in an airtight tin. Will store best in a cool place.

MAKES ABOUT 8

An early tomato jam recipe is an unusual and exciting discovery, especially among Grandma Roth's treasured "receipts." This spicy preserve was one of Grandpa's favorites and is surprisingly unlike the sweet bread-spreading substances we consider tomato jam today. Grandma's tomato jam is a spicy, acidy compote that is almost wickedly delicious, especially when served with roasted pork or old-fashioned country-cured ham.

⊷§ SPICED TOMATO JAM §⊷

9 *lbs. ripe tomatoes*
7 *cups sugar (about 3 lbs.)*
2 *cups cider vinegar*
Dash of salt

2 *Tbs. ground cloves*
2 *Tbs. ground cinnamon*
1 *tsp. ground allspice*

Scald the tomatoes in boiling water for 15 seconds. Cool under cold running water and peel. Remove the cores and chop coarsely. Put the chopped tomatoes, sugar, vinegar, salt, cloves, cinnamon, and allspice together in a large enamel* kettle. Set over a high heat and bring to a full boil. Reduce heat and simmer until a sheet forms across jam when a small quantity is dropped on a cold plate and allowed to cool. If you have a candy thermometer, the temperature for jelly is 220°F. Pour into sterile jelly jars and seal with a layer of melted paraffin. Let sit untouched until the wax cools.

MAKES ABOUT 6 PINTS

* *Note:* An enamel kettle is best used here as it is not affected by the acid from the tomatoes and vinegar.

The love apple's remarkable facility for blending well with other foods to create superb dishes has been used with great success in this recipe in which the tomato joins the apple and lemon to make a tasty treat. This jam is one of the most unusual tomato preserves and is an excellent breakfast spread.

⋐§ WAKE-UP APPLE JAM ૬∾

1 fresh lemon	*2 cups diced apples*
1 lb. can tomatoes or 2 cups	*3 cups sugar*
peeled tomatoes	

Put the lemon in a blender with a small amount of water and chop coarsely. If you do not have a blender, chop coarsely with a sharp knife. Add a small amount of water. Put the chopped lemon in a saucepan to boil until it is clear and tender. Add the tomatoes, apples, and sugar. Simmer gently until the mixture is clear and quite thick. It is best to use a candy thermometer for accurate testing. The temperature should reach 220°F. When cooked, remove from the flame and cool for 10 minutes. Stir several times to prevent the fruit from floating to the top. Pour into sterile jars and seal with melted paraffin. Let sit untouched until the wax has cooled.

MAKES 4 HALF PINTS

The Renaissance Italians called these delightful berries *pomi d'oro* or "golden apples," and likened them to the fabulous apple of discord that precipitated the Trojan War. It was a name that endured, and Italians have been calling love apples by that term ever since. These miniature yellow pear-shaped tomatoes are remarkably sweet berries, and in this fancy are combined with those other golden apples, the navel orange and lemons.

✺ GOLDEN JAM ❧

2 lbs. ripe yellow pear
   tomatoes
3 cups sugar

Juice of 2 oranges
1 Tbs. grated lemon rind
2 lemons

Scald the tomatoes in boiling water for 5 seconds, drain and cool by plunging into cold water. Peel each carefully. In a large bowl, arrange a layer of the tomatoes and top with a layer of the sugar. Repeat until all the tomatoes are used. Let stand in refrigerator for 8 hours or overnight. Drain off juice and mix with the orange juice and lemon rind. Bring to a boil. Reduce heat to medium and cook until the syrup will form a thread when dropped from a spoon. Add the tomatoes. Slice the lemons into very thin rounds. Add to the syrup and cook until the syrup is thick. Remove from heat and let cool for 15 minutes, stirring often so that the fruit will not float to the top. Pour into sterile jars and seal with melted paraffin. Allow to remain untouched until the wax has cooled.

MAKES 4 HALF PINTS

American sailors became the first of their countrymen during the latter part of the 18th century to taste an unusual Portuguese-made tomato sauce. It was a thick, spicy sauce with the ability to perk up monotonous shipboard fare. The sailors grew to love this sauce and called it "ketchup" after the more familiar mushroom and grape varieties. When they returned home the sailors told their women folk about the new sauce, and soon most of the sailors' wives, including Grandma Roth's forebears, were cooking tomatoes to duplicate the pungent sauce. It wasn't exactly like the Portuguese variety, but because of Yankee ingenuity, it turned out to be the superior product. We still call this "ketchup" or "catsup."

Grandma Roth had two varieties of ketchup, one which her mother had made and one Grandpa's sister was fond of.

◆§ SISTER'S KETCHUP SAUCE §◆

*2 gallons strained tomato
  pulp and juice**
*8 Tbs. pickling salt (large
  grain)*
1 tsp. cayenne pepper
¼ cup granulated sugar

2 pints cider vinegar
2 tsp. allspice
1½ Tbs. cloves
3 Tbs. ground cinnamon
4 Tbs. black pepper
6 Tbs. dry mustard

Put the tomato pulp and juice, salt, cayenne pepper, and sugar into a large enamel kettle. Simmer over a low heat. In a separate small enamel saucepan, boil for 1 hour the vinegar to which you have added the allspice, cloves, cinnamon, black pepper, and dry mustard. Strain the simmered vinegar through a hair strainer or several layers of cheesecloth. Add to tomato mixture and continue cooking until mixture is very thick or of desired consistency. Stir occasionally to prevent sticking or scorching. Spoon into sterile jars, seal; store in cool, dry place.

YIELDS ABOUT 6 QUARTS

* To prepare the tomato pulp, select ripe, soft tomatoes. About 1½ pecks (8 quarts) should suffice. Cut out all defective parts. Do not remove the skins. Chop tomatoes coarsely and boil in a large kettle for 1 to 2 hours until they are very soft. Use a food mill or sieve to remove all the pulp.

◆§ MOTHER'S KETCHUP §◆

*1 peck (8 quarts) ripe, soft
  tomatoes*
2 sweet red peppers
5 onions
1 garlic clove
1 large bay leaf
1 Tbs. salt

1 Tbs. whole allspice
1 Tbs. celery seed
1 tsp. cayenne pepper
*1 stick cinnamon, bruised
  and slivered*
½ cup granulated sugar
1 pint vinegar

Chop the tomatoes coarsely and put into a large enamel kettle.

Remove seeds from the pepper and mince fine. Slice onions into thick rounds. Slice garlic clove in half. Crumble the bay leaf into 3 or 4 pieces. Add the peppers, onions, garlic, bay leaf, and salt to the tomatoes. Simmer over low heat until tomatoes are very soft. Remove from heat and let cool for 15 minutes. Pass tomato mixture through a food mill or sieve; remove all the pulp.

Tie the spices in a cheesecloth bag. Return tomato mixture to the kettle. Add spice bag and sugar, and boil until thick. Stir often to prevent sticking or scorching. When of a desired consistency, add vinegar. Remove spice bag and discard. Boil the mixture for an additional 10 minutes. Spoon into sterile jars and seal.

MAKES ABOUT 6 QUARTS

An early American variation of ketchup sauce was tomato soy, spicier and of a thinner consistency than ketchup.

✢§ TOMATO SOY ℨ✢

24 large ripe tomatoes or	**2 tsp. cinnamon**
16 cups canned tomatoes	**1½ tsp. ground cloves**
4 cups cider vinegar	**1½ tsp. cayenne pepper**
3 lbs. sugar (7 cups)	**2 tsp. English mustard**

Chop the tomatoes coarsely and put in a large enamel kettle. Mix the vinegar and sugar, and stir until blended. Pour over the tomatoes, and add the cinnamon, cloves, cayenne pepper, and mustard. Place over medium heat and simmer gently for 3 hours. Stir often to prevent sticking or scorching. Spoon into sterile jars or bottles, and seal. Store in a cool, dry place.

YIELDS ABOUT 8 TO 10 CUPS

Chili sauce is another American adaption of a foreign sauce. It hardly resembles the Mexican variety except for its tomatoes and its name. With chili sauce, farm-style, the over-ripe, slightly spotted or bruised tomatoes, as well as those which were green or slightly green, could be used. This was one of the best ways to use those "entry way tomatoes," some of which ripened and some of which remained green.

◦§ CHILI SAUCE §◦

2 dozen large green tomatoes	*¼ cup salt*
1½ dozen ripe soft tomatoes	*¼ cup cinnamon*
1 dozen sweet green peppers	*2 Tbs. ground cloves*
8 large onions	*3 Tbs. ground ginger*
½ cup granulated sugar	*2 qts. cider vinegar*

Chop the green tomatoes coarsely. Scald the ripe tomatoes in boiling water for 10 to 15 seconds. Cool under cold running water, and peel. Cut out the cores, and remove any soft or bruised spots. Seed the green peppers and chop fine. Chop the onions very fine. In a large enamel kettle, combine the green and ripe tomatoes, the peppers, and onions. Add the sugar, salt, cinnamon, cloves, ginger, and vinegar. Stir until thoroughly blended. Put over a low heat to simmer for 2 or more hours until the sauce is thick and the tomatoes are very soft. Stir occasionally to prevent the mixture from sticking. Spoon into sterile jars, and seal. Store in a cool, dry place.

YIELDS ABOUT 5 TO 6 QUARTS

This chili sauce makes excellent, thrifty use of all those ripe tomatoes before they develop spots or imperfections.

◦§ RIPE TOMATO CHILI §◦

12 ripe tomatoes	*1 tsp. ground cinnamon*
2½ cups cider vinegar	*2 tsp. salt*
⅓ cup granulated sugar	*3 green Bell peppers*
¾ tsp. ground cloves	*2 large onions*
¾ tsp. ground ginger	

Scald the tomatoes in boiling water for 10 to 15 seconds. Cool under cold running water, and peel. Cut away any defective parts and chop coarsely. Combine the tomatoes, vinegar, sugar, cloves, ginger, cinnamon, and salt in a large enamel kettle. Seed the Bell peppers and chop fine. Chop the onions fine. Add to the tomato mixture and put all over a high heat, stirring constantly, until it comes to a full boil. Reduce the heat and simmer for 2 hours or until it is thick and does not separate after being stirred. Pack while hot into sterile jars, and seal. Store in a cool, dry place.

YIELDS 6 CUPS

Yankee sailors were also responsible for spurring interest in a number of delicious relishes made with tomatoes. "Chow chow," a pidgeon English word undoubtedly picked up by sailors in the Pacific, describes a tasty fancy which used sliced cauliflower, cucumbers, grated horseradish, and young, newly green tomatoes. This savory relish was spiced with vinegar and mustard, and was aged before being used.

CHOW CHOW

1 peck green tomatoes	1 oz. whole cloves
2 large head cauliflower	4 ozs. ground white pepper
2 dozen large ripe cucumbers	1 oz. stick cinnamon
	12 ozs. whole mustard seed
Grated horseradish	1 lb. ground mustard
2 lbs. onions	4 ozs. ginger
1 bunch fresh radishes	4 ozs. ground mustard
2 lbs. sweet green peppers	4 ozs. tumeric
3 sweet red peppers	vinegar

Slice the tomatoes into thick wedges. Slice the cauliflower into flowerets. Cut the cucumbers into large chunks. Grate the desired amount of horseradish, if you are able to get it fresh.

If using small onions, leave them whole. If they are large, slice each in half. Remove the leaves from the radishes, and trim away the tops and roots. Seed the green and red peppers and slice into halves or quarters as desired. Mix all the vegetables in a large crock. Sprinkle liberally with pickling salt (or table salt, if pickling salt is not available). Mix well and allow to stand for 6 hours in the refrigerator. If you haven't room in the refrigerator, pack ice with vegetables and keep in a cool spot.

Drain the vegetables and put in a large enamel kettle. Add the cloves, white pepper, cinnamon, and mustard seed. Add cider vinegar to cover and set on the stove to boil for 15 minutes. Moisten the ground mustard with cold vinegar and add to the vegetables just after removing from the flame. Do not allow mustard to boil in the vinegar. Let vegetables steep in vinegar and spices for 5 days.

At the end of 5 days, remove vegetables from vinegar. Add ginger, mustard (4 ozs.), tumeric, and enough fresh vinegar to cover. Put into covered jars to sit for 3 to 4 weeks before using. These pickles will keep all winter in a cool, dry place.

YIELDS ABOUT 25 QUARTS

A culinary touch from another land was all that was needed for American cooks to change a basic relish and create one with the tone and title of a faraway land. Mexican Relish is one such fancy in which American cooks have adopted the chili powder of Mexico and used it in a purely Yankee preserve. Excellent when served with a meatloaf or hamburgers.

⋐§ MEXICAN RELISH §⋑

2 cups cider vinegar	*1 lb. green tomatoes*
2 Tbs. chili powder	*2 green peppers*
2 tsp. dry mustard	*1 large onion*
Pinch of salt	

Heat the vinegar to a steady boil. Add the chili powder and simmer for 5 minutes. Add the mustard and salt. Chop the tomatoes. Seed the green peppers and chop fine. Chop the onion fine. Add tomatoes, peppers, and onions to vinegar mixture. Bring to a boil, pack in a large jar. Cover and let cool.

MAKES 1 QUART

Delicate seasonings, a gourmet's blend of pickling vegetables, and the judicious use of spices and herbs all contribute to make one of the most delicious of all tomato fancies, the famous India relish. This relish is probably adapted from sailors' reports of the many relishes and side dishes served at Indian meals.

⋅§ INDIA RELISH §⋅

4 green peppers	*Vinegar*
1 sweet red pepper	*1 Tbs. cinnamon*
1 piece horseradish root	*1 Tbs. nutmeg*
½ bushel green tomatoes	*1 tsp. allspice*
1 very large head cabbage	*1 tsp. celery seed*
3 lbs. onions	*1 Tbs. mustard seed*
2 cups salt	*3 lbs. brown sugar*

Cut the peppers open, remove seeds, and chop fine. Grate the horseradish root. Chop the tomatoes, cabbage, and onions. Sprinkle evenly with the salt and let stand in refrigerator overnight. If your refrigerator does not have room, pack ice in with the vegetables. In the morning, drain well to remove excess liquid. In a large enamel kettle combine the vegetables with vinegar to cover. Heat to a boil and drain. Add fresh vinegar, cinnamon, nutmeg, allspice, celery seed, mustard seed, and the brown sugar. Bring to a boil and cook for 10 minutes. Pack in sterile jars, seal. Store in a cool, dry place.

MAKES ABOUT 20 PINTS

ᏋᏏ SWEET TOMATO PICKLES ᏊᏋ

1 peck green tomatoes
6 large onions
1 cup salt
1 qt. cider vinegar
2 qts. water
1 gallon cider vinegar
2 lbs. brown sugar

½ lb. whole mustard seed
2 Tbs. ground allspice
1 Tbs. ground cloves
2 Tbs. ground ginger
3 Tbs. ground cinnamon
1 tsp. cayenne pepper

Slice the tomatoes into wedges. Slice the onions into thin rounds. Combine the two in a large kettle and sprinkle evenly with the 1 cup salt. Let sit overnight. In the morning, drain and press any excess liquid from them. In a large enamel kettle, combine vinegar (1 quart) with 2 quarts of water. Add vegetables and boil for 15 minutes. Drain.

While they are boiling, mix 1 gallon vinegar, brown sugar, mustard seed, allspice, cloves, ginger, cinnamon, and cayenne. Set on the stove and bring to a boil.

Pack hot vegetables into large jars. Pour over them the boiling vinegar and spice mixture. Run a knife around the inside to remove any air bubbles. Seal. Store in cool, dry place.

MAKES ABOUT 10 PINTS

Sour green tomato pickles were Grandpa's favorites. They were the last of the tomato fancies to be put up because they were packed with cabbage, which didn't ripen until long after the frost had hit the tomatoes.

ᏋᏏ SOUR GREEN TOMATOES ᏊᏋ

1 peck small green tomatoes
1 dozen onions
1 dozen large ripe cucum-
  bers
1 small head cabbage

1 cup salt
White vinegar
1 Tbs. ground cinnamon
1 tsp. ground cloves
1 tsp. black peppercorns

Chop the tomatoes, onions, and cucumbers. Slice the head of cabbage into thin strips. Cover all with ice water in which 1 cup of salt has been dissolved. Set aside to steep for 2 hours. Drain well and put into a large enamel kettle. Cover with ice water and let sit for 5 minutes. Drain again.

Pack the vegetable mixture into jars. Heat the vinegar (an amount sufficient to cover all the jars of vegetables). Add the cinnamon, cloves, and peppercorns. Let cool, then pour over the vegetables. Cover with airtight covers. Let sit for at least 1 month before using.

MAKES ABOUT 16 TO 20 PINTS

Vinegar-packed green plum tomatoes seasoned with garlic and aged with red hot pepper and dill are one of the most piquant vinegar tomatoes made. If you are daring, try these.

⋘ HOT TOMATO PICKLES ⋙

½ peck hard green plum tomatoes
1½ quarts vinegar
1½ quarts water
⅓ cup salt
⅓ cup sugar

2 garlic cloves, cut in thirds
½ cup dill seed
3 Tbs. mustard seed
2 Tbs. celery seed
1 tsp. crushed red pepper
1 Tbs. whole peppercorns

Wash the tomatoes and pack them whole into pint jars. In an enamel kettle, add the vinegar, water, salt, sugar, garlic, dill seed, mustard seed, celery seed, red pepper, and peppercorns. Heat to a boil, remove from the heat and let stand for 5 minutes. Remove garlic. Return brine to a boil. Ladle over the tomatoes. Run a knife around the inside of the jars to remove any air bubbles. Fill to the top with brine. Cover and cool. Store in a cool, dry place.

MAKES ABOUT 10 TO 12 PINTS

IX

The Gourmet Gardener

Sowing the seeds of love apples has become an increasingly popular activity among those who love the incomparable full savor of fresh tomatoes found only in the vine-ripened fruit.

There are ways to get tomatoes that are fresh, juicy, and wholesome. Your father-in-law might be a farmer, for instance, or you might live in tomato-growing country where the pick of the crop can be had for a mere pittance. For most of us, however, the only way to obtain fine, hunger-satisfying, old-fashioned, truly ripe tomatoes is by planting vines in our own garden patch.

Any convenient area can be a garden patch, ranging from a ten-inch clay pot for city dwellers to many feet of backyard growing space. Tomatoes can be as ornamental or as utilitarian as you like. Some tomato fanciers espalier their tomato vines in a formal garden scheme, while others allow the plants to languish *au naturel* and pick the fruit as it ripens on the ground. The wonderful part of being a gourmet gardener is that anyone can do it. There is a tomato vine designed for every locality and condition of residence, and every palate.

City farmers can place on a fire-escape or terrace several 10-inch or 12-inch clay pots with delicious cherry-shaped miniature tomatoes called "Tiny Tim." This variety is excellent for cocktails, salads, or succulent garnishes. The bushy plants grow eight inches high and 14 inches across. W. Atlee Burpee and Company thinks so highly of this particular variety and is so intrigued with the possibility of wooing more tomato growers that they are presently hard at work creating a larger fruited "Tiny Tim" type of tomato with superior quality and flavor.

For really dedicated city horticulturists there is a marvelous way of getting larger vine-ripened tomatoes from the window sill. The Burgess Seed and Plant Company offers an unusual hanging basket planter which can be hung from a fire escape or from an apartment terrace. This special planter uses no real soil. The vine grows in a clean vermiculite mixture and feeds upon a special plant food. These planters have been known to produce up to 80 pounds each of tomatoes, enough for a great many sauces, salads, and soups, with left-overs for assorted fancies.

The reason there are so many types of tomato plants is that the love apple is an easy plant to hybridize. Plant hybridizers find that from standard vines a tremendous variety of tomatoes can be produced. Plant historians, who trace the tomato back to a small wild vine growing in the Peruvian mountains, remark that it was at first simply a scrawny, berry-sized fruit. By means of selective breeding, it has now grown to its present portly prominence as a staple vegetable almost everywhere.

Gourmet gardeners can be grateful to the many seed houses who offer them a wide choice of exciting new tomato plants each season. These plants are geared to an epicure's palate. Such delectable sorts as Kabobs, a tomato grown exclusively for use in shish kebabs, are among the many selections. Special hybrid pizza tomatoes of the plum variety, such as San Marzano, Roma, and the Italian Canner are offered for those gardeners who favor southern Italian cuisine. For discriminating diners with a sweet tooth, there is a round cherry-shaped tomato so sweet that it is simply called Red or Yellow Sugar, for the respective skin colors. Juicy large eating tomatoes, firm plump stewing tomatoes, small delicate cocktail tomatoes—the varieties are so numerous that it would take a book alone to properly describe each member of the tomato tribe along with its various culinary attributes.

Color is yet another area in which the gourmet gardener can exercise choice. There are red, pink, orange, yellow and paper white tomatoes for horticulturists with an esthetic eye for bright gardens. Yellow tomatoes, the strain from which the Italians derived their name for tomatoes—i.e., *pomo d'oro*, or golden apple—is a delicious fruit which has a far milder flavor than most love apples. Contrary to popular belief, this yellow tomato is not less acid than its more blushing brethren. Color seems to have little to do with a tomato's degree of acidity, though a variety such as "White Beauty" is extremely mild and actually contains less acid than other tomatoes. No tomato, however, is entirely acid-free.

All tomatoes, despite their many differences are grown under the same general ground rules. They can either be started at home from seeds or bought as seedling plants from local nurserymen. Purchasing tomato seedlings is a simple, quick way to get tomato plants into the ground early. Seedling plants are grown in warmer climates or commercial greenhouses and shipped to nurserymen. Gourmet gardeners can beat nature by several weeks, using these seedlings to produce an early crop. The range of tomato seed varieties offered today is so great that many epicures prefer to grow several sorts themselves rather than to wait for plants to buy, unless they can be certain that the more unusual varieties of plants will be obtainable at local garden centers. This longer process is often well worth the effort, for the taste of tiny sugar tomatoes, delicately-flavored yellow pear tomatoes, thick-fleshed plum types, mild-flavored big yellow Jubilees, and the huge pink-red Oxhearts give great variety to the menus.

Tomato seeds are usually started indoors about six to eight weeks before the last expected spring frosts, which will vary with the climate. They may be set out safely after that time. Experienced tomato gardeners warn that it is often better to wait a little longer before starting tomato seeds because young seedlings tend to grow spindly and weak, and are less able to hold their own when set out in the garden. About a month before the last frost, they advise, is a good time to start seeds; the only exception being those of hybrid varieties which are usually slower to germinate than are standard varieties such as the Italian plum tomato.

Tomato seeds are set in shallow clay pots, flats, peat pots, or in plant bands set in flats. They may also be grown on in wood or plastic flats, which are shallow boxes with drainage holes in the bottom. The growing containers should be filled to about a half inch below the top with finely sifted, sterilized soil. Flats should have a sand or gravel layer on the bottom to provide drainage. Special seed-starting soil can also be purchased from garden centers and seed houses.

Because love apple seeds sometimes tend to rot when germinating, it is best to dust them before sowing with a fungicidal disinfectant. The seeds are then set in pre-dampened soil, in holes about ¼-inch deep. Two or three seeds should be sown in each plant band or pot or, for flats, in rows in little holes called drills. These can be made with a pencil. When the seeds are placed, cover them with soil and press it down lightly over them, then gently water the soil. The seeded containers should be kept evenly moistened at daytime temperatures of about 70° to 75°F., and night temperatures of no lower than 65°F. Some gardeners cover the pot or flat with plastic, held on with a rubber band, until green shoots indicate that germination has occurred.

Once the green seedlings nudge their way through the soft soil, place the containers in a sunny spot (after removing the plastic, if used), in temperatures of no higher than 75°F. daytimes, and of no lower than 65°F. at night. The soil should remain moist, but avoid overwatering, especially during cloudy, damp weather, to discourage the growth of fungi.

When the seedlings start to become overcrowded, soon after their first true leaves appear (these are the first leaves about the rounded pair which appear immediately after pushing through the soil), transplant them into individual peat pots or plant bands filled with soil, or into roomier flats. Set seedlings 3 to 4 inches apart in rows in the flats. Place only one plant in each peat pot or plant band, and set the pots or bands in a flat where they can be watered conveniently and handled *en masse* for shifting about. If seeds were sown directly in pots or bands, select the sturdiest plant from the several that appear; pull it out and discard the others. Keep the seedlings in strong light to make them short, strong, and bushy. Turn the container every few days and keep the plants from leaning toward the light.

As the weather warms and the love apple plants develop, they may be set outdoors in their pots to enjoy warm daytime sun, then brought back into the house for the night. This treatment will accustom the tender plants to outdoor conditions and lessen the initial shock of transplanting. However, this is not a necessary step.

When the weather becomes truly balmy (usually about the middle to the end of May in the North), the time has come to set the tomato plants out in the garden. Choose a spot that is very sunny, fertile, and well-drained. Tomato vines need plenty of water and nourishment to produce a healthy large crop of luscious love apples. Hybrids are particularly vigorous plants, once they start to grow, and need every bit of sunshine, water and food they can get, because they usually produce far more and better tomatoes than the regular varieties. Overfeeding, however, will produce more leaves and vines than fruit.

Before the vines are set, the soil must be well cultivated, and unless the soil is very fertile, cultivate in an organic-based commercial fertilizer, using about 3 to 5 pounds for a hundred square feet. For help in choosing the best fertilizer formula, a soil analysis may be useful. This service can be obtained easily from your County Agricultural Agent or your State Agricultural Experiment Station. For most gardeners, a 5–10–5 or a 4–12–4 formula works very well.

Gardener-gourmets are very careful when setting out these potential table delights into their permanent homes. As much soil as possible should be removed with each plant so as not to disturb the roots. Seedlings may be started in small square or round compressed peat pots. The entire pot is set into the ground and the roots grow through the pot. One excellent way to prevent the vines from feeling the full force of transplanting is to water each plant with a cupful of special starter solution, which can be made from the same fertilizer used to nourish the tomato patch. About three to four tablespoons of fertilizer per gallon of water are needed.

Unstaked love apple vines are set about three or four feet apart in rows four to six feet apart. If the gardener has a particularly green thumb and wishes to train the plant by eliminating all but one or two stems he can space the vines 1½ to 3 feet apart and set them in rows 3 to 4 feet apart. Really experienced gardeners, who love not only the fruit of the vine but the pleasant antique appearance of a well trained plant, grow the love apple vine as part of a formal garden arrangement. Tomato vines, patiently trained to grow on trellises, were highly popular garden ornaments during the 17th, 18th, and early part of the 19th century, and were grown more for their attractive appearance than for their fruit.

The training of tomato vines for better fruit, either on trellises or staked in a vegetable garden, begins when the plants form roots and begin vigorous growth. All side shoots should be removed as soon as they appear and the plant then trained to a post or wire support. Staked tomato plants take up less garden space and produce fruit with a maximum of Vitamin C content. Tests have shown that when the fruit is directly exposed to sunlight rather than hidden under thick foliage, a higher degree of Vitamin C is produced. An important point to remember in staking tender vines is that the main stem should be attached to the support by means of broad cloth tapes to prevent injuries that might occur if a wire or stiff twine is used.

Commercially grown tomatoes are not usually staked because of the time and labor it would take to prepare acres and acres of the vines. Instead they are allowed to sprawl on the ground, much like watermelon or cucumber vines. This poses a ripening problem. If the tomato ripens in contact with the ground it may rot. Mulching solves this problem. Mulch is a ground covering which holds the moisture in the soil and keeps the fruit away from the damp ground. There are many different types of mulches: grass clippings, wood chips, old cedar shingles, and peat moss, to name a few. Some farmers use a special plastic sheeting as a mulch. This black sheeting prevents weed growth by cutting off sunlight. It also keeps moisture in the soil by preventing evaporation, and, since black retains heat, the soil is 10 to 15 degrees hotter than it might be normally. Punctured plastic mulch is easy to water through and saves cultivating and staking tomato vines.

Growing tomatoes isn't all sweet flower buds and butterflies, however. Problems do arise, the most annoying being plant diseases and insect pests. Good old-fashioned garden practices such as putting the vines in different parts of the garden each year (crop rotation), keeping weeds down, and keeping the ground moist enough are usually all that is needed to insure a healthy and abundant late summer crop. Yet the tender plants are susceptible to the ravages of a few determined insects and plant diseases.

One of the most horrible looking of all insect pests is the squiggly tomato hornworm, which is a poisonous green. This ferocious little beast is noted for its ability to consume a great deal of tomato foliage in a very short time. The best way to fight this pest is to meet the enemy in hand-to-hand combat and pick each worm off the plant. Once the worms are destroyed in this manner, the plant is sprayed with a Rotenone preparation or other insecticide to destroy other chewing bugs.

Cutworms, another insidious destroyer, often attack the tomato as soon as it is set into the ground. The most effective weapon against these pests is a 3-inch wide collar (cut-worm protector) made of tarpaper or cardboard, which is put around each plant as it is set into the ground. A poison bait may also be set beside the plant to kill the worm. Poison baits are extremely lethal insecticides and should be kept away out of reach of children and household pets.

The other two major insect pests which dote on succulent love apple leaves are the aphis, a whitish-green or red sucking insect, and the flea-beetle, a small black insect that hops about from leaf to leaf making tiny pin-prick holes. These two insects are not only harmful because of the physical havoc they wreak on tomato plants but may also carry dread plant diseases such as fusarium wilt. The best way to stop these foragers from bringing a sad end to a crop of luscious tomatoes is to spray with insecticides which control sucking and chewing insects. Steady and preventative spraying of all plants is the best way to keep insects in check.

Plant disease is yet another matter. Proper choice of tomato varieties is one of the answers. Fusarium wilt, for example, causes wilting and yellowing of the tomato foliage. In areas where this disease is common, growing such wilt-resistant varieties as Heinz 1350, Manalucie, and Spring Giant Hybrid tomatoes, will aid in avoiding the malady.

Fungicides play an extremely important part in controlling plant diseases such as anthracnose and early blight which cause numerous spots and yellowing and drying of the leaves and stalk. These diseases are controlled by fungicides such as the Bordeaux Mixture. Late blight, a disease which occurs in damp summer weather, causes the blighting of leaves and dark watery spots on the fruit. Fungicides sprayed once a week during such weather will usually turn the trick.

Another common affliction of the love apple is blossom-end rot, caused by uneven water absorption by the tomato vine. This disease causes black sunken spots in the fruit starting at the fruit's blossom end. In order to prevent such a sad end to a vine-ripened tomato the gourmet gardener makes sure that his tomato patch contains plenty of calcium and composted organic matter and that it has good drainage.

Mulching plants is one sure way of preventing this disease. During droughts give tomato plants a thorough soaking once a week and avoid using fertilizers high in nitrogen. Nitrogen stimulates rank vegetative growth thus making tomato plants more susceptible to blossom-end rot.

Despite all these horrible possibilities (which must be listed, even though you may *never* encounter them—or, at most, one or two), tomatoes are one of the easiest and hardiest of all fruits to raise and are successfully raised by an ever-growing legion of gourmet gardeners each season. After all, for such a tremendous taste reward very little labor and time is spent on the average tomato patch. Is it all worth it? Just ask anyone who has ever tasted a slice of a garden-fresh love apple dripping with its own delectable dew.

Appendix

Tomato Tips

Newly married homemakers and bachelors attempting to ease restaurant bills by cooking at home are often very confused when they approach supermarket shelves and contemplate an awe-inspiring variety of canned tomato products. As they face row upon row of cans of stewed, puréed, peeled, juiced, and concentrated tomatoes the thought passes through their minds that all these canned tomatoes can be put to some kitchen use . . . but how?

The tomato's versatility is to blame for this common confusion. Love apples can be used in so many different ways that commercial canners have merely taken care of many of the preliminary cooking steps needed in preparing fine tomato recipes. This convenience is a tremendous help to the person who may not be cooking a dish at the proper season or who may not have the right amount of tomatoes on hand to use in a recipe. The following list gives an explanation of what can be done with the most common canned tomato products.

TOMATO SAUCE—This is the most popular form of canned tomato and has innumerable cooking uses. There are two types of sauce, Spanish and Italian. The most frequently used type is the Spanish style sauce. The Italian type is commonly used for pasta dishes. Basically, tomato sauce is a seasoned tomato purée.

PEELED TOMATOES—This is the second most popular form of canned tomato and is used in sauces, pizzas, soups, stews, roasts, and casseroles.

CANNED SALAD TOMATOES—Tomato wedges and a specialty item called baby tomatoes are now being canned commercially for use in salads, eating as is or any other way you would use fresh tomatoes. Nothing could possibly surpass fresh tomatoes but, if they are not available, canned salad tomatoes make surprisingly good substitutes. The secret to their use is to make certain that they are very, very cold.

STEWED TOMATOES—This can be a side dish by itself or used to enhance casseroles, gravies, and roasted meats. It is one of the most common tomato products.

TOMATO PURÉE—This is obtained by sieving tomatoes so that seeds and skins are separated from the pulp. This sieved product is simmered down until it is slightly thickened. It contains no seasoning and is used for sauces, soups, and stews.

TOMATO PASTE—This is a highly concentrated tomato purée. It is most frequently used to make tomato sauces of various consistencies. The chef adds his own liquid to the paste, obtaining just the right thickness of sauce to suit his culinary purpose. Much of the tomato paste sold in this country is imported and sweetened with fresh basil. Many American packers of tomato paste omit basil because domestic tomato paste tends to be sweeter than the imported kind.

TOMATO JUICE—This tomato product is made by pressing steaming hot tomatoes through fine mesh screens. The resultant juice is free from skins and seeds. It is salted and hermetically sealed in cans or glass jars. Tomato juice is high in vitamin content and low in calories, and it is drunk as a cocktail and is useful for making aspics, soups, casseroles, and sauces.

Gourmets, who love their tomatoes cooked to perfection, have discovered that by adding a teaspoon of sugar to a can of cooking tomatoes they are able to make the flavor of the canned tomatoes approach that of summer-fresh love apples. They have also discovered another interesting canned tomato livener, monosodium glutamate. By the addition of this popular Oriental aromatic, the taste of tomato products, such as tomato juice and ketchup, is improved.

What many people fail to realize about canned tomatoes and fresh tomatoes is that they are interchangeable. Often, when the fresh fruit is not stocked on the kitchen shelves, a cook has to put canned tomatoes in a salad. If you want to use canned tomatoes to the very best advantage this way, make sure they are well chilled before serving. If a recipe calls for canned tomatoes and you have only fresh ones on hand, use 1⅓ cups of seeded, peeled, and chopped tomatoes, which have been simmered for 10 minutes, to equal one cup, or 8 ounces, of canned tomatoes.

Often a cook might feel at a loss when he runs across a recipe which calls for tomato juice, and he has none on hand. A can of tomato paste will make a decent substitute if it is diluted with four cans of water. A teaspoon of sugar, dash of salt, and some monosodium glutamate will even transform the paste into a drinkable beverage.

A host will find canned tomato juice an extremely handy pantry item for parties. Use it for a really great Bloody Mary Cocktail: 1 jigger vodka, 2 jiggers tomato juice, a dash of Worcestershire sauce. Shake well with cracked ice, strain into an Old Fashioned cocktail glass with a cube of ice.

Canned tomato paste may lend a rather bitter taste to a tomato sauce. This bitterness can be eliminated by simply frying the paste in a bit of oil for 2 to 3 minutes over medium heat. Constant stirring will keep the paste from scorching or sticking.

Many beginning cooks are more experienced with canned tomatoes than with using fresh fruit in preparing recipes. Vine-ripened, freshly cooked tomatoes, however, are one of summer's rare table treats, and they are very easy to prepare.

Peeling is often called for in recipes and tomato skins can be removed very easily, simply by immersing them in boiling water for 15 to 20 seconds and immediately plunging them in cold water or putting them under cold running water to cool. Their skins will then easily slip off. When peeled love apples are to be used in sandwiches or salads, slice them with the core to retain the juices in the fruit. Plum tomatoes and beefsteak tomatoes have tender skins and are not usually peeled for sandwiches or salads. After peeling, tomatoes are often seeded.

Seeding a tomato merely means that it is sliced in half against the core, and the inner pulp with the seeds is removed, leaving only the thick tomato flesh. Often tomatoes are seeded over a fine sieve so that the juice can be saved and added to the recipe. Tomatoes are usually seeded when they are to be used in long-cooking sauces because the seeds, when simmered for a long while, tend to give the sauce a bitter taste.

Often tomato recipes are needlessly spoiled by the cook's not knowing what to do under emergency conditions. Not all tomatoes, canned or fresh, are the sweetest of their clan and despite a carefully followed recipe, which might have turned out perfectly many times before, there is always a chance that an accident could occur. Here are a few tricks that can literally save the sauce.

BITTER SAUCES—At times tomato sauces suddenly turn bitter because of simmering too long. They can be saved by the addition of a modest amount of sugar (a teaspoon is usually enough). Taste the sauce to see if the bitterness has been reduced.

SALTY SAUCES—"If there is too much salt in the sauce," an old saying proclaims, "the cook must be in love." When faced with an over-salted sauce the best thing to do is add a large, peeled raw potato, which has been halved, and simmer it in the sauce until done. The potato will usually absorb the excess salt.

THICK OVER-COOKED SAUCE—If you are distracted for several hours and forget that a tomato sauce is simmering on the stove, the results can often be a purée-like, viscous mass. Don't despair. The sauce can be thinned down, without too much damage, by adding water to it.

Index

THE BRASS-TACKS ENTREPRENEUR

THE
BRASS-TACKS
ENTREPRENEUR

JIM SCHELL

HENRY HOLT AND COMPANY / NEW YORK

To Mary,
my friend, business partner, and wife,
who encouraged me to rediscover
a long-forgotten love affair
with the written word.

Henry Holt and Company, Inc.
Publishers since 1866
115 West 18th Street
New York, New York 10011

Henry Holt® is a registered
trademark of Henry Holt and Company, Inc.

Library of Congress Cataloging-in-Publication Data
Schell, Jim.
The brass-tacks entrepreneur / Jim Schell.—1st ed.
p.   cm.
Includes index.
1. New business enterprises—Management.   2. Small business—
Management.   3. Success in business.   I. Title.
HD62.5.S33   1993
658.4'21—dc20   92-32399
                                                            CIP

ISBN 0-8050-2370-4

First Edition—1993

Designed by Katy Riegel

Printed in the United States of America
All first editions are printed on acid-free paper. ♾

10   9   8   7   6   5   4   3   2   1